Ant

1940, the son of an Indian Army officer and his wife.

After following his father and stepmother out to South Africa in 1948, he was educated at Hottentots-Holland High School in Somerset West, in the Cape Province.

He returned to the UK in 1963, and eventually spent 22 years programming main frame computers, before he and his wife retired and moved to East Devon in 1999, where they have lived ever since.

Letters home from The Raj

By Anthony Cuerden

AUSTIN MACAULEY PUBLISHERS™

LONDON • CAMBRIDGE • NEW YORK • SHARJAH

A CIP catalogue record for this title is available from the British Library.

ISBN 9781786290519 (Paperback)
ISBN 9781786290526 (Hardback)
ISBN 9781788231893 (Ebook)
www.austinmacauley.com

First Published (2018)

Austin Macauley Publishers ™ Ltd.
25 Canada Square
Canary Wharf
London
E14 5LQ

Forward

The letters & poems in this book were written by my mother, Margaret Mary Cuerden (nee Beal) from 1936, when she returned to India after education & secretarial training in England, until her untimely death (from appendicitis) in November, 1941.

She was born on 16th September, 1914 in Darjeeling, in India, the first child of the second marriage of her father, Hastings Evelyn Beal (to Marguerite Cooper), whose first marriage ended tragically when his first wife died shortly after giving birth to their only child, Thetis, about whom I know absolutely nothing.

My mother had three other siblings. Phyllis, Edward (aka Teddy), & Angela. I believe the last named is still living, though sadly in a nursing home, in Pittsburgh, Pennsylvania, USA.

Hastings Beal (1883 - 1962) was an official in the ICS (Indian Civil Service - sometimes known as the "Heaven Born"). According to my stepmother, he was at one time being considered for the Viceroyship of India. How true this is, I do not know, as I understand he was somewhat given to exaggerate his own importance!

My father, Henry Ballantine Cuerden, was born in Woolwich on 4th October, 1908, the elder son of Major George Edward Cuerden, & Matilda Charlotte Cuerden (nee Ballantine). He had one brother, Lewis. He was educated at Taunton School & Sandhurst Military College, after which he joined a Gurkha regiment in the Indian Army. This is probably where he obtained the nickname "Daju", which my mother mentions him by in some of her letters. I understand that the Nepalese, including the Gurkhas, don't address each other by personal names, but call each other "elder brother", "elder sister" etc, as the case may be. Strangers, visitors &, in the case of officers in Gurkha regiments, are likewise addressed so. "Daju", I understand means "elder brother", so I presume this is how my father came to acquire it. He attained the rank of Lieutenant Colonel during WW2, but had to retire from the Indian Army after Indian independence in 1947. He died of a heart attack in October, 1951, in South Africa.

I have left the letters & poems exactly as I found them - ie all the typing errors, grammatical errors, & misspellings etc are all as found in the original letters & poems. I felt that leaving them in situ would make the book more authentic.

The photographs are also as I found them, with no identifications, as, apart from the one of my father in uniform, annotated "Wana NWFP" (which stands for North west Frontier Province), but undated, none of them have any annotations.

Anthony Cuerden,
Metcombe,
Devon,
January 2016

S.S. Mulbera

26th September 1936

BRITISH INDIA
· LINE ·

Dear Mummy,

Thanks awfully for your
letter. We got it at Port Said,
and missed the one at Malta.
We're awfully glad Mrs. Milner is
coming, it will be companionship
for you. We had a letter from
Daddy at Port Said, too. He
hadn't much news, except that he

2.

hadn't been well again.

We posted our last letter before we reached Malta, so of course you haven't heard what we did there. We arrived in the evening, and a large party hired cars and drove to a bathing beach 12 miles from Valetta. Maltese drivers are quite insane! The roads are bad, with ~~fierce~~ hairpin bends, and the cars pretty ancient. The drivers take the corners on two wheels and seem to prefer driving with the headlamps switched off. We discovered half way there that our car had no brakes, the driver stopped by going into reverse! One car was smashed up in a collision

3.

but nobody was hurt.

Port Said is a good spot! We had a grand time there. We went ashore about 3 p. m. with Jim Manson and two other padres (in good hands, you see!) and bought topees at Simon Artz. They cost 3/6 each. Then we bathed. Back to Simon Artz, where we met Freddy (that's Gordon's nickname - I mentioned him before - he's the most amusing lad on board) and a crowd. I joined up with Freddy & his crowd and Phyllis stayed with the padres. We went different ways after that, so I'll tell you what my crowd did. We went to one or two of those fascinating open. air cafe's

4

for drinks and hors d'oeuvres. They give you marvellous hors d'oeuvres, and they're included in the price of the drinks. We met the Captain who joined us and stayed with us till midnight. He's rather jolly. We finished up the evening at the Eastern Exchange. We arrived too late for the cabaret but were in time for two or three hours dancing. We got back to the ship at about 3 a.m!

29. 9. 36.

We had the concert last night. It was a good show, but my word it was hot! We've had a following wind all the time we've been in the Red Sea, so you can imagine the heat! There were rather too many passengers in the show

BRITISH INDIA
· LINE ·

S.S. ....

....

5.

who thought they could sing, and got
up on their hind legs and proved they
couldn't ; otherwise it was good.
Phyllis & I were in a play "The
Mermaid's Curse". This was acted
silently to music — no speaking. The
first scene was the navigating bridge
of the S.S. "Morebeary." A mermaid
(Phyllis in green, crepe paper, with silver
scales painted on — she looked wizard)
lay asleep in the background. Captain
Slocum Bustion paced up & down. The

6.

mermaid awakes, and attracts the Captain's
attention. She tries to entice him away.
He does a little dance with her and
kisses her, but suddenly remembers his
duty & flings her away. She rises
and calls down curses on the ship.
Curtain.

2nd Scene. The Purser's Office.
Percival Perseus the Purser and Sherlock
Blake the detective or Professional
Snooper are discovered sitting at a Table.
In the background is a large notice
board headed "Lost". Enter a dear
old lady (Freddie in a grey lace
dress S a white wig!) who indicates
that she has lost her specs. A notice
is pinned up, & she is led off.
Enter, in great agitation, a girl who
has lost 10/-. Next entry, Slim

7.

Adams, eating a banana. He grabs the Purser's sandwiches. A notice is pinned up under the "Lost" — "GIRLISH FIGURE

Enter: a passenger who has lost his braces. His trousers fall down, revealing red & yellow pants. Next entry: myself, weeping. I indicate that I have lost my engagement ring. The Purser comes over to console me. I weep on his shoulder. He moves away to make out a notice, but I grab the lapel of his coat & pull him back. He consoles me very well, I cheer up. While we are doing our stuff, Sherlock makes out ●notice "Lost - Engagement Ring" and pins it up. I wink at the Purser & tear it down. The Purser pulls a

8.

bunch of rings out of his pocket, I choose
one, he puts it on the engagement finger.
& we do a little dance. Enter the
Captain, who has lost his entire outfit,
attired in a barrel! Curtain.

3rd scene. The Swimming bath.
Enid & I, after a quick change, are
mermaids. We do a swaying, arm-waving
dance, then start playing with the pile
of things that were lost — specs, braces,
etc. Phyllis dances in the Captain's coat.
We laugh & play with that. We
suddenly hear something, dive into the
pool & disappear. In comes Sherlock
disguised by a wig, beard & specs.
The mermaid splashes him. He becomes
suspicious & dives into the pool. (Slim
made bubbling noises into the microphone

S.S. _____

_____

9.

when Sherlock was supposed to be
swimming , the effect was marvellous)
Sherlock dives , brings up the braces;
dives again & comes up struggling with
Phyllis. She pulls off his beard,
& promptly changes her mind, & starts
because without the beard he is good-looking,
vamping him ^ They dance. She
suggests that he should come away
with ^her They dive together & disappear.
Curtain . Finis .

10.

People have started sleeping on deck now, men on the starboard side ladies on the port side. We slept out ~~bed~~ last night. The worst of it is you have to be up at 5.30, to leave the deck clear for cleaning. But it's well worth it, all the same; our cabin is almost unbearable, even with a fan going, because as it's on the starboard side we have the sun on it all day. The heat isn't knocking us up, though, we're still full of beans, and in anything that's going!

I hope Teddy & Angela will take this letter for themselves

11

too. If I wrote to them separately
I would only repeat this letter; and
one letter to all saves postage bills!!

Has Angela started school yet?
I do hope she will write and tell
us all about it, and what friends
she is making. Has Teddy been to
any more Proms? We often say to
each other "I wonder what they're
doing at home now?" and try to
picture it.

Are you keeping really fit &
well, mummy darling? & not
working too hard? And is Mrs. Milnes
with you now? If she is, give

12.

her my love.

Love to ~~Ted~~ Teddy and Angela
and your self.

Mary.

P.S. The ship's overdue at Aden,
and we are ~~exp~~ expected to
be 3 days late at Calcutta!

This is due to cargo delays
at Malta & Port Said, also
we took about 16 hours through
the Canal instead of the normal
10 hours.

TELEGRAPHIC ADDRESS:-
"CONCORDIA"
TELEPHONE Nº 108 REGENT.

UNITED SERVICE CLUB,
CALCUTTA.

19ᵗʰ October 1936.

Dear Mummy,

Thanks for your letter,
it was lovely to find one
waiting for us when we
arrived. We actually arrived
about 3.30 on the 16ᵗʰ, just
three days late. I picked
out Daddy ages before I
could really see his face!
He doesn't seemed to have
changed an awful lot; still
as tall and spare as ever,

2.

just beginning to grey, but not very badly. He wears specs. all the time now.

The flat is lovely, two big bedrooms, a sittingroom and a large verandah. Each bedroom has its own bathroom attached. Daddy hasn't been in the flat more than a few days, so it isn't quite straight yet. The hot water comes from geysers, which Phyllis and I thought rather an alarming idea, but we find they are very simple to work, and almost fool-proof, so you are not likely to hear

Letters home from the Raj

3.

of us being blown downstairs!

Do you remember some people called Hare Duke at Palgrave Mansions? Diana Hare Duke used to teach Angela dancing. Well, she is out here now, we met her yesterday. Her father is a very old friend of Daddy's. Isn't it extraordinary? On board we met a Captain & Mrs. Deane, who turned out to be friends of Daddy's. They had known him for years in Barrackpore.

Daddy is going to invite quite a lot of people to a tea dance on Nov. 6th, the first dance at the Club after the

21

4

Poojah holidays. A kind of "coming-out" for us! Tea-dances are very different out here, and go on till 8 o'clock.

Freddy is going to be in Calcutta for a fortnight, then he sails for Australia. By the way, Freddie is Gordon Challis! He doesn't look like a Gordon, so he got nicknamed Freddie on board, because that name suits him perfectly. I am going to a flick with him to-night. He will be back from Australia in 3 months time, when he will be promoted to 3rd Officer on a mail boat between Calcutta and Rangoon,

TELEGRAPHIC ADDRESS:
"CONCORDIA"
TELEPHONE Nº 108 REGENT.

**UNITED SERVICE CLUB,
CALCUTTA.**

6.

so I shall be seeing him again before we come home.

Tim and Alan came to see us after dinner yesterday. They leave to-morrow for up-country, somewhere. Raddy described them as "worthy, but dull"; my own opinion exactly!

Oh, dear, we were tired the day we arrived! The night before everyone had been giving farewell parties in their cabins. I went to a few of them, and

6.

didn't start going to bed till 3 a.m.!

Belinda is a darling, a great fat friendly animal, blandly indifferent to orders. ¾ cocker-spaniel; the rest is an unknown quantity! Angela would love her.

By the way, when is Angela going to write? Teddy's letter was very much appreciated. I will write to him by the next mail. We are sending this air mail, so that you may know we arrived safely

7.

and in good health, but in future we will write by ordinary mail.

Sorry about the cook, better luck next time! It's grand to hear that you are so much better you don't even need charcoal. Must be the relief of getting rid of two troublesome daughters!

We are simply dying to see your photograph, I do hope it arrives soon.

Lots of love
from

Mary.

28, Stephen's Court,
Park Street
Calcutta.
28ᵗʰ Oct. 1936.

Dear Mummy,

We're already having a marvellous time with crowds of invitations — at least I am, poor Phyllis has been in bed for a week with a cold and a temperature. Too bad, isn't it? But I think she'll be up in a day or two now.

2.

I had an absolutely grand time last night. I went out to dinner with a friend of Daddy's, called Norman Calder, a middle-aged man, but rather amusing – definitely a bit of a lad. There was another lady there and a boy called Arthur Legat. After dinner we went to Firpo's, which is <u>the</u> place for dancing here (apart from the clubs). Firpo's closed at 1 a.m. so we went on to a night club, where we stayed till three. I have fixed up to

3.

meet Arthur again. One invitation always seems to lead to another!

Last Saturday Norman took me to the races at Tolleygunge – a perfectly lovely place – and was I thrilled! I lost and won alternately till the last race, when I was all square. Then I had a hunch about a certain horse, a rank outsider, Norman advised me against it, but I insisted on backing it, and we shared a tote ticket. It won easily and paid 30 chips! 15 Rs. each for

4.

Norman and me – about 22/- in English money!! Norman won about 230 Rs. altogether, and as he says I brought him luck, he is taking me again next Friday. Phyllis is going out in a party with him next Saturday, if she is well enough. I am going out with Freddie that night. Freddie sails for Australia next Wednesday.

Daddy and I are going down to the docks to-morrow after tea to see Freddie's new ship. Phyllis won't be able to come, but

5.

a girl we made friends with on board is coming to sit with her while we are away.

We are quite settled down now and beginning to pick up a little – just a little – Hindustani. Our daily programme is something like this. Get up at 6, go to the 6.30 mass, come back to chota hazri, at 7, go out again with the dog, for a good long walk on the Maidan until breakfast at 8.30. Then I type and Phyllis attends to matters such

6.

dhobi, mending etc., till 11.30 or
twelve, when we go out in the car
shopping or meeting people for
drinks somewhere. Tiffin at one,
then sleep till 4.30 – teatime.
Then out again, either for a walk
or in the car till 6 or 6.30, when
we bath and change. Dinner is
never before 8.30, and between
7 and 8.30 is the really sociable
hour of the day – people either
call at the flat or we go to
the Club or other people's houses.

7.

After dinner there's generally something doing. People are still away, a good many of them, for the Puja holidays, but they finish this week, and then Calcutta will begin to get really full.

Rather a pity Mrs. Milner has to go, as the old girl's money must have been rather useful, but of course it was definitely not worth it if she's such a nuisance, and a strain on your nerves. I bet Teddy's pleased!

8.

Give my love to Angela, and tell the young imp to write to us some time!

Lots of love

from

Mary.

28, Stephen's Court
Park Street
Calcutta.
29th Oct. 1936.

Dear Teddy,

Thank you very much for your letter. I'm afraid you're going to be awfully right about "going to India to see the land, and seeing the season!" But Calcutta hasn't got much to show in the way of temples and suchlike, though there is a Jain temple we

2.

intend seeing some time. Poor old
Phyllis is missing everything; she
has had a very bad cold for the
last week, and is still in bed
with it.

I have already been to one
race meeting and won 15 chips,
equal to 23/-s.! The man I was
with won 230 chips, and is taking
me again to morrow as a mascot!

I have been out to two or
three dances and one or two flicks
already, and I am booked up

3.

solidly for about a week ahead,
and a few stray invitations after
that!

But one thing I do miss very
badly is the wireless. Good concerts
are very rare here, I am told.
The hotel bands only play light
stuff, and that not too well, though
they are not bad for dance music.

Calcutta is a very untidy place.
I picture a really curlized town
with broad streets and fine
buildings. It has those, but

4

flocks of goats in the streets are an ordinary sight, and one may walk peacefully along, and suddenly find oneself surrounded by cows! Also huge grey bulls roam the streets unattended and generally ignored, often standing in the middle of road broadside on to the traffic, of which they take not the smallest notice, or lying down on the pavements when and where they choose, so that one has to step over or round them.

Lots of love from
Mary.

28, Stephen Court,
Park Street,
Calcutta.

17th March, 1937.

My dear Mummy,

Thanks for your letter, but I am hurt that you should again complain of not having heard from yme. I really have NOT neglected you to that extent! and since Phyllis left, I have been a model daughter, and written regularly every week. Perhaps my letters have gone astray, though I can't think why they should: I'm sure I always address them properly.

My job is going along nicely, and as I told you in my last letter (if you got it!) I am being kept on by the firm. It has turned very hot, which makes work a little tiring. We have now reached the stage when one discards all bed-clothing, and puts the fan on full blast. However, I am keeping well, in fact I feel amazingly fit, so I am evidently one of the lucky ones whom the hot weather suits.

I went riding two days ago, and fell off again taking a jump. Every time I take a jump I must confess I am in a blue funk, since I fell off the first time. This time I hurt my back somehow, wrenched or strained it, so that I was ignominiously carried off by the Sergeant, and had to spend the day in bed. I am quite all right now, and mean to go riding again to-morrow morning. I shall probably be a little nervous next time I jump, but not so bad as I used to be, because last night I met an awfully nice man called Harry Cuerdun (pronounced Kirdun) who had been in a cavalry regiment, and he gave me some good tips on jumping, so I feel I may do better next time.

Harry is now in the Fort, attached to Mechanical Transport, and has a fleet of Ford V.8 s to look after. We took one out last night on the Barrackpore road, which, as you may know, is dead straight for about 12 miles. The bus did 75 mph with ease! It was lovely, and so cooling on a hot night.

Eric Kitchin may be coming down for Easter, which would be fun. After Easter Calcutta will be pretty empty, nearly all the girls I know are either going home or to the hills for the hot weather!

I don't know how much longer tennis will last, It's getting rather hot for it already, but I still play regularly at week-ends.

Give Teddy my love, and tell him that I heard a perfectly lovely gramophone record the other day. The piece was called "The Enchanted Lake", and it was played by the Boston

- 2 -

Symphony Orchestra.   I wonder if he knows it.   I will try to find out the name of the composer so as to let him know.

I enclose a short note for Phyllis.

One of Phyllis' best friends out here, "Chubby" Chapman, is leaving Calcutta at the end of this month, so we asked him to come round about peg-time to-night, and have asked a few people in too.   It began by just being a "good-bye" to Chubby, but has developed into a positive cocktail party!

My love to Angela, and tell her to be good.

Lots of love,
from
Your affectionate daughter,

Mary.

J. B. L
CALCUTTA.

Java Bengal Line
7.1, Clive Building
Calcutta
8ᵗʰ April '37.

My dear Mummy,

    Just a short note to prove I haven't
forgotten you — I am too busy to spend my
lunch hour typing letters to you and Phyllis.
Thanks for your letter. Don't worry about
the eyes. They are O.K. now, and my
reading glasses aren't too revolting, in
fact they have rather fetching pale pink rims.
Daddy actually sails a week to-day!
I just can't realise it, and don't
think he can either. I go into the YWCA
next Tuesday, but may not stay there
long, as Elizabeth Young said how
much she would like me to stay with her,
but we haven't heard her father's

2.

opinion on the matter yet, nor how much they will charge. I'm going out in a party to-night and Elizabeth will be there, so I hope to find out more and let you know by the next mail. As for trams, I'm not going to get a chance to use them so far as I can see, because Raju (Harry) will take me there and back as long as he is in Calcutta and Johnny will when Raju has gone.

I've been played quite a lot of tennis, and am going straight on to tennis after work to-day, to play at Major & Mrs. Waddell friends of Raju's in the Fort. No more riding since the ride with Eric I probably mentioned in my last letter, but I am riding next Sunday with Johnny.

Lots of love to everyone, more news next time.

Tons of love
Mary.

Galway House,
　　Middleton Row,
　　　　Calcutta .

15ᵗʰ April 1937.

My dear Mummy,

　　　　Here I am in the Y W C A, and settling down quite happily. I must confess I was as miserable as blazes the first night, in a tiny bare cubicle, but now I'm sorted out, with a few photos about, it looks quite homey, and it's all much comfier than I expected. There's a lovely big lounge downstairs, with enormous "sink - in - & - can't - get - out" sofas and cuddly cushions, magazines, and a ping - pong table!

　　　　got to-day off from the

2.

as Daddy sails at 5, and have been busy unpacking & tidying things up while Daddy has dashed round seeing banks, & tiresome business things like that. Daddy & I had a sentimental little farewell dinner-party for two last night, with Daddy continually murmuring "I wonder how you'll get on in Calcutta?" and myself replying "I wonder how you'll get on in Sutton?"

I'll be all right, I've had a bit of luck finding someone to take me to and from work.

The drawing's going along fine. Raju told Johnny that I was without exception the quickest learner he'd ever met. Raju has gone up to Darjeeling. He received a warning

3.

notice the other day to hold himself in readiness to go to Waziristan any moment. So he went to Darjeeling to say goodbye to his best girl before he goes to war.

I wonder if you realise how serious this Frontier business is? Do the papers say much about it at home? 6 British officers were killed the other day. I forget exactly how many, but lots have been killed since the beginning of the year.

Please ask Phyllis to forgive me for not writing her a separate letter this week. I am so tired after all this packing and unpacking and the rushing round generally during the last few days. I'm expecting Daddy any minute now. Love to everyone.

Lots of love, Mary.

P.S. Snap is of me & Daju at the
Swimming Club. Not very good
I'm afraid. Daddy is bringing
you home another snap.
mB

The Y. W. C. A.
Middleton Row,
Calcutta.
21st April. 1937.

My dear Mummy,

Thank you very much for your letter.
I'm glad you liked the sketches of my fellow
workers — some of them. Just lately I have been
doing a lot of that at parties — it's very
popular and makes the party go.

The quiet time you mention didn't last
long! I've been having a marvellous time during
the last month. And <u>please</u> don't worry about
my being here by myself — it's much pleasanter
than being on my own in London would be.
The heat doesn't worry me, the Y.W. is quite
comfortable, I have lots of friends and go out
nearly every night, and I am taken to and
from work in a most luxurious car!

I've joined the Swimming Club and

2.

spend quite a lot of my spare time there. Sometimes I go there for a bathe before breakfast. Bill Blomefield calls for me in his car and takes me down. Bill is a friend of Johnny's, and a very nice lad. Unfortunately he is going away soon. I have been going out with him a lot. He travels for some stationery manufacturers — same sort of firm as Cooper, Dennison & Walkden. He spends about a fortnight here every two or three months. Johnny is another person I go out with a good deal.

Rajn is in Darjeeling at the moment, but is coming back next week - if he isn't called up to Waziristan in the mean time.

Eric has promised to send me a gramophone and some records — highbrow ones — but they haven't arrived yet.

Love to Teddy and Angela.

Lots of love
from
Mary

The Y.W.C.A.,
Middleton Row,
CALCUTTA.

27th April, 1937.

My dear Mummy,

Thanks for your letter. The one to Daddy I
will forward to Port Said. It makes me laugh, to be
frank, to read that you don't like the idea of my staying
on by myself. What is the fuss about? I'm living most
respectably at the Y.W., Work equally respectably during
the day, and am (still respectably) entertained one way
or another most nights.

I enclose three snaps taken at the Swimming
Club the other day. The lad in the topee is Bill
Blomefield, whom I have already mentioned. I can't
think what has happened th the snap showing a general
view of the Swimming Club, because it looks so flat and
dull, whereas we took the snap because the Club was so
lively and jolly that day. Still, it gives you some
idea what the place is like.

I have been going down to the Swimming Club a
lot before breakfast, and sometimes go back to the Great
Eastern Hotel for breakfast with Bill, Hugh and Ross.
The new boss is there, and the other day I had the honour
of giving him a lift to the office! These Dutchmen are
comic, I thought he was never going to stop bowing when
he thanked me for the lift. However, it probably made
a good impression on him!

Col. Vining has offered to let me ride his polo
pony, Bubbles, and the other day I went to try it. He
had just been playing polo on it, but only a couple of
chukkas so it wasn't tired. I said I'd get up just for
five minutes to try her, but she behaved so badly that I
stayed on for over half-an-hour, till I had got her to
obey me. I got her under control in the end, but it was
quite a job. These polo ponies are on their toes the
whole time, and the wretched animal never stopped dancing
and prancing for a minute. Very spectacular, but she's
not a bit vicious or dangerous. Anyway, I can manage her
now, and can ride her when I like. Col. Vining insists on
coming with me for the next ride or two, but he says after
that I can ride her quite alone.

28.4.37.

       I am going to ride Bubbles again this evening when I get out of the office.

       Daju has come back from Darjeeling, and still doesn't know whether or when he'll be sent up to the war.

       Eric has sent me a gramophone and stacks of records, all very high-brow ones, Debussy, Brahms, Bach (I told him not to send Bach), Wagner, and a Dvorak's "New World Symphony", also a Concerto by Thaikovsky. There is an entire Mass Cantata by Bach, on dozens of records, which I don't intend to waste my time by playing. It's a great relief to be able to put on something good, when six-months' old dance records are being played in the cubicle next door.

       My love to Teddy and Angela.

               Tons of love

                  from

                    Mary

29. 4. 34.

    Rode Bubbles yesterday and had a grand ride, we were galloping all out – and by jove she can move! Then we met some ditches, took 3 in grand style, but she pecked at the fourth and off I came. Not a bit hurt. I hope to ride again to-morrow.

                        May

13th May, 1937.

My dear Mummy and Phyllis,

I suppose by the time you get this Daddy will either
have arrived or just be on the point of coming. What thrills!
Give him my love, and I will include him in my mail home from
next week on.

What a little scamp Angela is! Tell her from me
she's a bad, bad girl, and if she doesn't look out I'll come
home to look after her - and give her my love. She'll enjoy
Daddy's fairy stories, if Phyllis hasn't told them to her
already.

Coronation Day was the grandest fun. We had a
whole holiday, of course, and all the important buildings,
and several private business houses, were flood-lit, and the
ships on the river,were twinkling with little lights, and
decorated with lighted signs of the Crown & Cypher and things
like that. The crowds were terrific, of course. We had a
marvellous party at the Saturday Club, given by Major & Mrs.
Windle. Daju, Mac, and Stella were among the party, and
Elizabeth Young joined us later. Our costumes were grand
and the little red-white-&-blue pill-box hats were an
absolute riot. The King's broadcast came through very
badly, I haven't read the paper yet, so don't know what
he said! The Saturday Club went on till 2.30, then the
merrier element in our party got together and went on to
the 300 Club (I was the leader in that movement!) That
goes on as long as anyone's there, and there were crowds
last night. Oh, dear, am so sleepy to-day! When I have
finished work I am going riding again, too, so I shall be
pretty tired by to-night (and won't go out to-night for
anyone).

It's awfully hot now, one is dripping most of the
time. However I am very well, and full of energy, as you
can see! and I've lost a terrific amount of weight to my
huge delight. I am now 8 stone 12 lbs, and if you remember
I was always 9 stone 8 lbs. at home. I just can't get over
being under 9 stone!

The Y.W. is going along quite nicely, but I got
ticked off (very nicely, but still ticked off) for coming
in at 5 in the morning about a week ago. The rules don't
allow any later than 1.30, which I haven't the remotest
intention of taking any notice of. I told the Manageress
so, and she quite sympathised, but said 5 o'clock was a bit
too much. However, Coronation Night was a special concession
so there won't be a row about that.

I'm awfully keen to hear your accounts of this Coronation business at home.   Did Phyllis go with the Murdochs, or whoever it was, to see the procession?   Did you see the flood-lighting in London?   And how did you celebrate?

Duty calls.

Love to all.

                    Tons of love from

                                Mary

18th May, 1937.

My dear Mummy,

Thanks so much for your letter, I'm awfully sorry I missed the last mail, and hope you weren't worried.

It's really rather a relief that you should have seen my letter to Phyllis after all, because you do know how things are; I couldn't make up my mind whether to tell you or not, but apparently you knew already.

Traffic in Calcutta practically came to a stand-still last week during the Coronation Floodlighing; masses and masses of babus all out with their families to stand and stare! Awful business; took about half-an-hour to go a hundred yards. But my word, what fun Coronation Night was! We had a large party at the Saturday Club; but I think I told you in my last letter what a success our costumes were, and how there was dancing outside as well, ir the rather pretty garden, and how some of us went across the road to the 300 Club, and how both Mac and Daju got distinc merry and how I discovered I had lost half a stone in weigh Daju is usually T.T., but came off the T.T. standard for suc a special occasion. Elizabeth Young was in a different par at first, but joined up with us later. She has given me a permanent invitation to stay a night at her house at any tir which solves the late-night problem at the Y.W., because if I know it's going to be a late party, I simply tell the ᴵ.W. manageress I am staying the night at the Youngs.

It's pretty hot now, though actually the temperatu is not so high as it has been, but the humidity has gone up terrifically - 71%.

I went to a tiffin party with Richard Parker and George Golding the other day, and someone in the party told me I belonged th the A.D.S. (the Amateur Dramatic Society). I said I didn't. He said yes, I did, he'd elected me on sight! I believe they have their next show in July; I'm looking forward to that, it should be fun.

Did I tell you I'd had yet another accident on a horse? I remember telling you how I came off Bubbles. A week later Col. Vining hired a horse for me to ride while he was playing polo on Bubbles. We were quietly cantering down the side of the Maidan when the horse suddenly tried tc turn on to the road. I pulled her round sharp and came slap bang up against a low branch! Off I came, and hurt myself in an awkward place, so that I had to take a cushion to the office with me the next day! To everyone's huge

- 2 -

delight, of course.   But what **really** annoyed me was, when
I got up again I was shaking so much I had to dismount
promptly, and next time I rode I was distinctly nervous.
Daju is taking me in hand now, and training me in Sandhurst
fashion - no stirrups!   He is also making me stay inside
the School till I get my confidence back.

See how well I'm being looked after?   People
teach me riding, and driving, take me to and from the
office, give me scent, flapjacks and eye-lotion, and even
take me to the doctor when they think I ought to be
inoculated against something!

The girl who used to do the coding and de-coding
of telegrams has suddenly left because she's got a better
job, so I'm doing her work now.   I don't find it too much,
and hope very much they will let me go on doing her work
as well as mine, instead of finding another girl, then I
can say I'm doing two girls' work, what about a spot more
salary?   Rather a good scheme, don't you think?   Though
of course it would make my hours a bit longer.

My driving is O.K. now, though I haven't done
much parking yet.   Daju says I'm the quickest learner he's
ever met.   I love driving, even in Calcutta with its
wretched half-witted babus, and cows, and bullock-carts.

Must do a spot of work now.   Love to all.

Your loving daughter,

Mary.

3rd June. 1987.

My darling Mummy & Daddy,

Only time for a very short letter. I do feel so awful about forgetting Angela's birthday. Please soothe her down for me and assure that I will try to send her something by the next mail. I haven't had much time for shopping because one of the girls in the office left suddenly and I've been working overtime.

An awfully funny thing happened yesterday at the Y.W. At dinner I sit next to an Indian woman, who turned round to me last night and said "I've just heard your name is Beal

(margin, top): & Raju takes me riding in the evenings after work sometimes, but since three falls I haven't ventured astride the school, & won't till ? regain confidence – which is sadly lacking at the moment!

(margin, left): P.S.S. I've been good about beat-ups – they've been finishing at the 5!! I still bathe instead of about 2 or 3 a.m. 2 or 3 times a week. I've been good about how more reasonable

2.

Was your father by any chance H.E. Beal of the I.C.S. and your mother Marguerite Cooper?" I nearly fell off my seat! Mummy, do you remember "Bunnie", or The Rajkumarie of Kakira? Because this was her, and she remembers you and your music-lessons very well, and sends you her love. Isn't it funny? She was only a kid then of course, but she remembers you saying you were engaged, and writing to her after you were married. Now she's married herself, and apparently separated since she lives at the Y.W. She said her marriage wasn't happy, so of course I didn't enquire any further. She hopes you are well and has your photo in her room! Also one of me as a baby!

Lots of love
Mary

P.S. Don't tell me it's a small world, or I'll scream!

J. B. L.

CALCUTTA.

13, Camac Street,
CALCUTTA.

14th June, 1937.

My darling Mummy,

I have got the most thrilling news for you - I'm sure
you're going to be awfull y pleased. Can you guess-? I have
just got engaged to be married! I wonder if you have an inkling
who it is. Well, it's Daju - otherwise Harry Cuerden, who has
just been transferred from the 7th Ghurkhas to the Royal Indian
Army Service Corps, and gets his Captaincy in January. The
transfer means more money, and as he is due for home leave at
the end of next February, we hope to get married as soon as he
becomes a Captain, and sail home together. Won't that be just
marvellous? I am so thrilled and happy. We won't have much
money, but enough to manage on. After his leave he will be
stationed in Allahabad.

Just imagine it, all being well, next time you see
your eldest daughter she will be a staid married woman! Isn't
it incredible! You'll like Daju - everyone does. And we agree
about people usually, don't we? We both liked Dick Maddocks, for
example, and both detested Carlos! I am sending a snap of Daju
and me and some others by ordinary mail. It was taken at the
Swimming Club, and we are all being funny with hats, but it will
give you some idea of what he looks like. He's an ugly little
devil, as a matter of fact. But we've been grand friends ever
since we met three months ago. Since then we have met almost
every day, except for ten days when he was in Darjeeling. And
during the time we have known each other, he has been frightfully
keen on another girl, and I had a heaving hop on another man -
Bill Blomefield, who was very good-looking, but I soon got tired
of him - and all the time we were keen on different people we still
went out with each other and told each other all about things, and
went on being the best of friends. And I do think that being as
good friends as that before we fell in love means that we have a
pretty firm foundation for our love and for our happiness, don't you?

We got engaged on Friday evening last, bought the ring on
Saturday afternoon, and had the most hilarious celebration party on
Saturday evening. The ring is a beauty. A cluster ring, with a
sapphire in the middle and diamonds round it.

I want a military wedding. Don't you think that would
be jolly? Crossed swords and all sorts of fun like that. And
P hyllis could come to stay with me as a married sister, wouldn't
she? I think that would be awfully good for her.

Daju is a Presbyterian, but he isn't making any fuss
about religion, though he doesn't think his mother will like it
very much having Catholic grandchildren. On the other hand, his
brother married a Catholic, so she already has Catholic grandchildren

So she ought to be used to it!

J. B. L.

- 2 -

CALCUTTA.

As a matter of fact, Daju is pretty broadminded about religion, and thinks a good many Catholic ideas very sensible - he believes in Purgatory, for example, which he should do as a good Presbyterian.   NOT

We went round to see Richard Parker yesterday afternoon, and stung him for tea, while we broke the news. Apparently he had rather expected it, although he has only met Daju once. He seemed awfully pleased. It seemed by what he said to be rather a relief to him I hadn't got engaged to Eric, whom he regards as a milksop - which nobody could call Daju. He's only met Daju twice now, but I rather think he likes him. He promptly said we must go and have dinner with him one day, so we are going to-night, and he has asked some other people and it's going to be quite a party. Nobby Clark is throwing us a party on Wednesday, Captain & Mrs. Elsdon Smith are giving us one on Saturday, Terence Shiels wants to give us one, in fact everyone seems to have greeted the news with the utmost enthusiasm!

If only you could be here for the wedding! You said in your last letter how much you'd like to come out for the next cold weather - I wonder if you will possibly be able to manage it?

With lots and lots and lots of love

Mary

18, Camac Street,
CALCUTTA.

23rd June, 1937.

My darling Mummy and Daddy,

By now, of course, you have heard the great news and
have had time to discuss it at length. How I wish I could be
with you to talk to you about it. I am longing for your letters
in answer to my airmail one. It's grand fun being engaged, and
everyone seems awfully pleased about it, and not nearly so
surprised as we ourselves were! Richard Parker gave us a little
dinner party the other day; I rather think he approves; he
seemed to like Daju.

We have now booked our passage home next year in the
name of Captain & Mrs. Cuerden! We are coming home on the
"Viceroy" which leaves Bombay on 2nd April, and we are flying
back to Calcutta by K.L.M. That passage is booked too. We
shall have about 3½ months at home as we are flying back, as the
K.L.M. planes only take 3½ days from London! Phyllis can't
beat that with her old Imperial Airways planes, can she?

I do think it's so splendid Phyllis should have got a
job. I bet she's bucked about it. Is she being paid well?

Daddy's letter, in which he reminded me to go and see
Belinda must have crossed mine, in which I told him I had been
to see Belinda and her puppies, and she nearly went crazy when
she saw me - almost licked me away! I am going to take Daju
out to see Belinda one Sunday. Theo Thorne would approve of
Daju as he is T.T.

A few days ago I wasn't at all well. I hadn't been
feeling too good for about a week, so I went to see Mac, who
gave me a tonic and told me not to take so much exercise. He
forbade me to ride or swim or dance for four days. The four
days are over now, thank goodness! but I am still going to bed
early every night - Daju returns me to my digs most punctually
at 10.30 or 11, no later. I must say I feel a different person
for it. I think it was largely due to reaction after all the
excitement.

Everyone is saying these are mighty queer rains we're
having. It rains less than it did during the little monsoon.
We have a storm about once a week, and the rest of the time, it's
sunny as blazes and hot as hell.

- 2 -

I expect you'll be awfully surprised, Mummy darling, to hear that I have actually become quite keen on bridge! The Keegan girls play it a lot, with a rather nice man called Garth Williams, and myself for the fourth. Sometimes Daju comes along and takes a hand, too, but he's not much good. I suggested to him he should take some lessons from you, but he seems a bit nervous about getting dragged into really serious bridge. I also want him to take some dancing lessons. So you see I am not too prejudiced - I can see room for improvement in him!

There isn't much to tell you about when I lead such a quiet life. You'll be glad to hear, however, that my digs. are comfortable, the food is very good (in fact I'm putting on weight again), and my bearer speaks good English, and is most efficient.

Bye-bye for the present,

and lots and lots of love,

from your very loving daughter,

Mary.

18, Camac Street,

CALCUTTA.

24th June, 1937.

Dear Teddy,

Daddy mentioned a letter you were writing to me in
his letter, but it has arrived yet.   I suppose I've got the
sack now as Calcutta Correspondent!

How's work going?   When do you get your annual
holiday and what do you propose to do with it?   I believe
ages ago someone told me you meant to take a trip up the Rhine,
or something equally thrilling.   Send me a picture-postcard,
please, if you do.

I won't say anything about my engagement, because I
expect you're sick of hearing about it by now.   But you'll
probably enjoy meeting Daju - being in the Army you'll be able
to have one of those discussions, so dear to your heart, about
Pacifism and Disarmament and Is War Necessary, etc.   He may be
one of the "brutal and licentious soldiery" but he isn't hide-
bound like most Army people.   Do you approve of Phyllis' Air
Raid course, and efforts in the Peace Shop?

Have you seen any good shows, or heard any good
concerts or read any worth-while books?   Remember when we're
home in April we'll expect you to tell us what to see and do
In London Town, because we've got to crowd into three months
all the shows and concerts and ballets and opera (if possible)

- 2 -

that we possibly can, because we'll be four years in
Allahabad, far, far from such delights.

Duty calls.   I must go and take down some
letters.

Cheerio, and don't think I've forgotten you
because I write so seldom.   Do you ever see Thetis?
Because if so, give her my love, and tell her my conscience
allows me no peace for not writing to her, but I really,
truly will do so as soon as possible.

Lots of love,

from

Mary.

P.S. Isn't it just marvellous, Angus's mother has just cabled her approval and loving greetings ! Sounds as if I'm going to have a nice mother-in-law !

18, Camac Street
Calcutta.
30th June 1937.

My darling Mummy and Daddy,

I haven't yet heard your views on this engagement business; if you replied airmail, as the occasion deserved, I expect to hear from you about it next ~~week~~ Saturday. Incidentally we have decided we can't wait till February, so the wedding is now fixed for 5th October. We have discussed all this with Richard Parker. If the firm allows it, I shall go on working. Otherwise we'll be rather hard-up.

I don't know at all how Daddy's book is going. There's been no review in the "Statesman" or else I've missed it. But I've kept a look-out.

There's been no letter from Mummy the last mail or ~~two~~. I suppose with Angela in bed and Phyllis working

2

all day she's much too busy. I'm glad
Angela's better. Has she gone back to
school yet?

Eric Kitchin came down to Calcutta
yesterday. I went out to lunch with him,
and he asked me and Raju to have tea
with him at Tollygunge when I came out
of office. It's such a lovely, quiet,
green place. Eric and Raju were rather
funny; they were so polite to each other.
I burbled nonsense most of the time,
because as soon as I stopped, these two
made such painfully stilted conversation.
I went out to dinner with Eric last night,
and met oceans of friends, who all
stared very hard, so I suppose the rumour
will now go all round that Raju and I
have quarrelled! But that will be
contradicted by the announcement which is
to appear in the "Statesman" in a day

3.

or two.

Poor Barbara is in bed with dengi or dengue (or however you spell it) fever. So we are short-handed at the office, but luckily are not busy enough for that to matter. There's an awful lot about, which I am told is usual this time of year, and also masses of mosquitoes, which I am told is not usual for this time of year. Mac showed me how to distinguish between a malarial mosquito & an ordinary one. A malarial mosquito never wears a football jersey; the harmless ones do.

Incidentally Mac will be best man if we marry in October; he is going home on leave in November. Oh, dear, you'll get so tired of my harping on one subject!

Lots of love
from
Mary.

J. B. L.

CALCUTTA.

18, Camac Street,
CALCUTTA.

5th July, 1937.

My darling, dearest Mummy,

       Weren't you terribly thrilled by my news? Everyone else
seems so pleased, to judge by the letters I got. Perhaps you wrote
such a long one it missed that post! So I shall look for one by the
next mail.

       I enclose some snaps taken of Daju and of us together.
I'm positive you'll be pleased now you see what he's like - don't
you think he's got a thoroughly <u>nice</u> face? And rather good-looking,
too? Of course, he is only a penniless subaltern, but if I can keep
on my job after we're married, we manage all right; and by January
he'll be a Captain, and then I won't even need my job, unless I want
to go on working.

       The date is now fixed for the 1st or 2nd October. By the
way "Living in sin" doesn't mean marrying without his C.O.'s permission,
as Daddy seemd to think; it means marrying under age, so he doesn't
get marriage allowance. Marriage allowance will begin when he's 30.
He is now 28. His Colonel does know, and thoroughly approves. I
have met the old bird once or twice, and he's quite amiable. As a
matter of fact he told Daju that "getting engaged was the best thing
he'd done for years - he had improved tremendously since it happened".

       Angela's letter was delightful - do tell her so. It made
Daju howl with laughter. By the way, hasn't my present arrived,
because there's no mention of it? Angela should have it by now.

       There's practically nothing to tell you, because we have
gone strictly into purdah in order to save up! But we had quite a
nice time when Eric was here. He took us out to Tolly on Sunday
morning, and took me out by myself once or twice. He and Daju got
on much better after the first meeting or two. Eric is going to try
to come down for the wedding, but isn't sure yet if he can.

       Lots of love, Mummy darling, (and
remember I'm dying to hear what you've got to say
about it all).

from

[signature]

18, Camac Street,
Calcutta.

12th July, 1937.

My poor, darling Mummy,

I am so terribly terribly sorry to hear how things
have turned out. It really is too awful, and I can well
imagine the bitter shock and disappointment to you. It is
difficult to understand, too, because he was always telling
us how wicked he thought he had been, and how much he wanted
everything to be put right again. There is no doubt about it,
that awful Pamela woman must have got hold of him again.
Don't believe a word of that about only seeing her twice for
business; I discovered after Phyllis had gone, that when I
was safely out of the way at a party, he used to take her out.
Richard Parker and Mr. Hare-Duke both told me that; and I
would rely absolutely on the word of either of them alone.

About money. Even if he does cut you down to £350,
don't Phyllis and Teddy both contribute a little? You have
only one lot of school fees to pay now. Also I have been
discussing the matter with Daju. You can imagine a young
subaltern hasn't much money, and he has no private means, but
he always sends <u>his</u> mother something, and don't see why we
shouldn't send you something too. We really ought to able to
manage it when he gets his Captaincy, anyway. We can really
only get married if I can keep this job or get another one, but
if I do have a job, we won't be so badly off, and it's my money
to send to you if I want to. If I can send you anything, I
damned well will, and Daju is in absolute agreement with me
about it. He is such a perfect darling. It may not be much,
Mummy darling, but with contributions from us and Phyllis and
Teddy, surely things won't be too bad. So please, please
don't worry because that will only make you ill, and then
matters will be worse, which won't do at all, at all.

Of course the whole trouble with Daddy, which I'm
afraid we have to face, is that he has developed religious mania,
and I really don't think he's quite responsible for his actions.
To be mean about money is one of signs; one of the little
peculiarities that go, queerly enough, with religious mania.
And he has some queer mental kink which enables him to reconcile
his fanaticism with his extremely irreligious actions.

- 2 -

I am in bed at the moment myself, but don(t worry, it's nothing serious. I had violent toothache quite suddenly on Saturday morning, and went to a very clever little Japanese dentist that afternoon. I have never seen such an immaculate surgery! He told me that a nerve had become exposed and the tooth must come out at once. I blithely said O.K., thinking it would take about ten minutes, and it took 1½ hours! They had to give me a second local anaesthetíá, because it took so long the first one wore off! They pulled and pulled and pulled, taking it in turns, then the top half came off, so I knew I was in for a good time. But they were very clever just there, and did a little operation, cutting the roots in half, so that they could pull out one prong at a time. And discovered one prong was hooked, so no wonder the wretched tooth wouldn't come out! Of course my mouth was as sore as blazes after that, I can't eat anything solid yet two days after, and as I swallowed a lot of blood my tummy is upset. So I amlazing luxuriously in bed. We're very slack at the office these days, they won't miss me. Barbara Keegan explained matters to Mr. Broeksma, who is rather a dear, and he was most sympathetic, apparently.

I'm writing airmail because I wanted you to know as soon as possible that you are not to worry, because we'll all look after you.

Lots and lots of love, Mummy darling.

Mary.

Excuse typwritten name, my pen is at the office.

18 Camac Street,
Calcutta.

31st July, 1937.

My darling Mummy,

        Thank you for your airmail letter in reply to
my ditto. As for not allowing us to make such a "sacrifice"
- be blowed to that - we'll see. Anyway, the point is, you
are to remember that with all the perfectly good sons and
daughters you've got there's no need for you to worry; you've
got two sons now, with Daju. I admire tremendously the way
you write that you are determined to manage - you certainly
have got guts. I'll ask Richard Parker your question next
time I see him. Incidently I told him all about things a
little while ago, and he pointed out that Daddy can't just
reduce your allowance when he feels like it, even if we are
over age, he has to get an Order from Court to cut out the
children's allowance. If he does so without that Order,
you can take up the matter with your solicitors. Richard
said that if Daddy goes to Court about it, or if you do
through your solicitors, our allowances are sure to be cut
out, but on the other hand, your personal allowance would
almost certainly be increased. That is what Richard says,
and he knows all the legal ins and outs; remember he's been
a judge. So you see, Daddy can't just play about with your
allowance as the fancy takes him.

        Please excuse the messiness of this letter, the
typewriter ribbon is playing merry hell.

        I hope you haven't been awfully worried because I
missed the last three mails. I -

I'm afraid there won't be a hope of us helping you during the first year at least. We have been working things out !

This wretched course in Pindi will lose us quite a lot of money during the 3 mths in Pindi & I, of course, will lose 3 months wages by going up with him. But of course I must go, because we will only have been married about 3 months then, & simply couldn't be separated as soon as that !

Daju won't get Calcutta allowance

2nd August.

      Back at work, so I've got a decent typewriter.
As I was saying, I missed the first mail because I was in
bed with a touch of dysentery, and didn't want to worry
you about it. After a day or two on an arrowroot diet
(filthy stuff!) I was all right again and went back to
work, only to return to bed about three days later with
dengue fever! So the next mail day I had a temperature
of 104°, and wasn't up to much, let alone letter-writing!
Then one day when I got out of my bath, I fainted three
times right off, and had an awful job getting dry and
getting into a nightie and back to bed; I was half-fainting
the whole time. The doctor was horrified, and said I had
no business to be getting out of bed at all, but as I pointed
out, I only had a bearer, and had to wash myself! But when
Barbara Keegan heard about it, she promptly said I must come
and stay with her, so that her ayah could look after me, and
along came Dick Colquhouh, a great big chap, wrapped me up
in a rug. carried me out to the car and took me along to
Barbara's, where I stayed till I was all right again.
And here I am back at the office, with oceans and oceans of
work piled up waiting for me. Barbara is in a nursing home
herself now, with dysentery and some obscure germ which seems
very difficult to get rid of.

J. B. L.

CALCUTTA.   - 2 -

         As for Daju looking after me - you ought to have
seen him pinning my arms down, and making me swallow nasty
medicines! Your confidence in him is absolutely justified.

         How perfectly ridiculous of the Convent to make
such a fuss about Angèla staying away! She obviously couldn't
go if she wasn't well.

         I had a congratulatory letter from Miss Hornsby by
the last mail, which i thought was very sweet of her.

         Daju has just heard that he is due for Rawal Pindi
at the beginning of next January, so we are driving up there,
leaving on Boxing Day, probably. Won't that be fun? We'll
be about ten days on the road, and will see lots of India,
Delhi, Lucknow, oh, lots of places, we worked out our route on
the map. We'll take it in turns to drive, and stop at Dak
bungalows, and the dog will come with us. We'll be there
till the 9th April, when he is due for leave. We have now
decided to fly home and come back by sea, instead of the
other way round, and will leave Karachi by K.L.M. on (I think)
the 16th April, arriving in London four days later! But I'll
let you know definite dates later.

         Lots of love, and please forgive the gap in my letters.

*P.S. See Phyllis' letter for
full description of
wedding dress".*

                        Your loving daughter,

                         Mary

P.S.   On reading your letter again, I find I have not answered
       all your questions. Pamela has definitely left Calcutta.
       In fact she sailed about five or six weeks ago, and left
       me an address in Folkestone - a bank address. (This was
       so that I could write to little Peter, of whom I was very
       fond; poor kid, think what an awful position he's in!
       and I should imagine she leads him an awful life).
       Pamela tried very hard to get friendly with me, but I
       managed to avoid meeting her, though I spoke to her on
       the 'phone sometimes when I wanted to see Peter.

       The other question. Daju has seen your photograph, and
       ~~remarked that you~~ looked rather stern - it does make you
       look definitely severe, ~~doesn't it?~~ - ~~but~~ I explained that
       was just the photo, you aren't like that a bit, really.
       He was very pleased at your suggestion that we should stay
       with you first of all, and says may we stay with you for
       as long as a fortnight, when we first arrive? He will
       get a car as soon as possible, and we plan some nice
       drives for you! And he has also been enquiring about
       your taste in shows, thrillers, musical, or what? So
       just hope and pray that nothing happens to our leave,
       because it's all going to be so lovely.

18 Camac Street
Calcutta
12th August 1937

My dear Teddy,

Thanks a lot for your letter and good wishes.

Your holiday in Germany sounds marvellous. I bet you can speak German well now. Germany must be one of the loveliest countries in the world, with its forests and rivers and old castles. The people sound delightful.

I expect we'll enjoy England as much as you enjoyed Germany. You've no idea how one feels almost sick with longing out here for smooth lawns, and mellowed houses, country lanes with primroses on the banks, castles like Bodiam, for example, peaceful and dreamy with lilies in the moat and gorse, a blazing yellow on the Downs. There is no spring in Calcutta and no autumn merely a cold weather, a hot weather and the monsoons (which means hot and damned sticky weather, rain every day almost) all of which probably sounds rather silly to you, but one's memory pictures of England that is paradise!

All the same, England is nice to look at, not to live in. I prefer the life out here. It is so much friendly, informal and being engaged is great fun, though of course that would be the same anywhere! We are busy choosing wedding presents, buying my trousseau, working out our future budget and making endless plans. And always being invited to have drinks before dinner (the most sociable time, when everyone drops in on someone else) by people who want to congratulate us and wish us luck. I have had to give up riding because getting married is expensive, also I have had fever and too much exercise isn't good in this sticky heat. I'm not as sorry as I might have been because I had a lot of falls!

You will like Daju. It will be fun coming home next year, his leave has just been postponed again (the army is like that) but we hope to arrive in England about the beginning of June (provided nothing else happens). Would you mind waiting till then for a Christmas present? By Christmas we will still be struggling to pay off various wedding expenses, such as honeymoon expenses, new clothes, etc.! Any idea what you would like?

Soothe Phyllis down for me because I didn't write to her this week. It really was your turn though! Love to Flip and Angela.

Please give mummy a message I forgot to put in her letter. I hope to send some enlargements of the snaps of me and Daju by the next mail. I haven't been able to see about them before as I was ill.

Much love
Mary

                                        18 Camac Street
                                        Calcutta
                                        19th August 1937

My dear Mummy,
        Please tell Phyllis not to give me such awful
shocks! I found her cable waiting on my desk this
morning, and when i started de-coding it, the very first
word meant "very anxious" My first thought was "mummy's
ill!" Of course, the next word "no letter" explained
matters but my hands shook like aspen leaves for half an
hour afterwards!
        I know I missed 3 mails, but cannot understand
why you had no letter for 5 weeks, anyway, for goodness
sake don't get het up when I don't write, if anything went
seriously wrong, YOU WOULD HEAR AT ONCE I promise you
that. I am terribly sorry you have been so worried.
And here are the enlargements, one of us together
and one of me, it's rather a nice one, so I thought you'd
appreciate that, too. I also attach a cutting from "The
statesman" our announcement. It would be a grand idea
to put it in the "E'bourne Gazette" as you suggested.
You will notice 2 mistakes, Daju put it in and he has
described me as an "elder" instead of "eldest" daughter,
and forgot the "Margaret". You will notice he is the
R.I.A.S.C, not the 10th Ghurka riffles he transferred to the
Corps because the pay was better.
        I am frightfully busy so please forgive this short
letter. See Phyllis' letter for all my news such as it is.
Love to Angela and Teddy.
                    Your very loving daughter
                            Mary

P.S. I can't tell you how sorry I am you should have been
so worried. But Daju looks after me so well, you really
have no need to be anxious.

18 Camac Street
Calcutta
26th August 1937

My darling Mummy and Phyllis,

One letter between you because I am pressed for time, which you will not be surprised to hear after my last letter in which I explained, I believe that we might be going to Pindi early in September, and therefore everything has to be got ready for a wedding on the 2nd September instead of 2nd October. Imagine the rush we've had the last week or so, and we STILL HAVEN'T HEARD! Aren't Headquarters just the limit, because we'll have to start for Pindi next week if he's due there on September 13th driving takes about 10 days, you see.

Mummy's last letter has made me realise why you got no mail for five weeks. You mention an airmail letter. I wrote airmail 2 weeks running, I think, so for 2 weeks of course you got no ordinary mail and on top of that I missed 3 mails when I was ill. But for goodness sake don't get so het up when you don't hear from me. If I'd been seriously ill you would have heard from Daju or Richard. Besides, it might have occurred to you that we'd be busy choosing trousseaux, wedding presents going to the cocktail parties people gave for us, etc. And dash it all Daddy also writes frantically demanding letters, Phyllis likes her own separate letters, that means three letters to the family alone and lately I've had congratulatory letters to cope with too. I simply can't keep up a copious correspondence all my life, can I? I simply hate you to be worried like that but it's too silly that you should be worried! Dash it all, I'm nearly 23, will be married in a month and have a absolutely reliable unofficial guardian, Richard, So what IS the fuss about? Next time I get a cable I won't write for another month! And won't answer the cable! I won't be treated like a baby.

Don't take all this too much to heart Mummy. I'll try not to miss so many mails again, honest. But being proud of my independence, it peeved me to think you thought I wouldn't be all right.

I think I have answered most of your questions by now, but in case I've missed out any please wait till we get home to give us a present. You see, we shall be living in boarding houses and hotels until our leave, so don't want too much stuff to cart about and store, we won't need much household stuff until the next time we're out here and settle down to housekeeping. Daju's mother also means to give us linen and silver, she has a lot she doesn't use, so better wait till we can all get together and not duplicate things. By the way, she lives quite near in Wimbledon, 24 Cambridge Road Wimbledon I've been meaning to give you her address for some time but kept forgetting it. She lives by herself, Major Cuerden died a few years ago and the other son is married.

So glad Auntie Bar has got a job at last it sounds rather a good thing.

G ive my love to Rosemary.

What did you think of the enlargements? Pretty good weren't they? And while I remember it my wedding dress is not satin after all, the cheap satin didn't look nice and I couldn't afford the good ones. So it is in a very attractive white material with a sort of watered silk effect, a rippled pattern you know what I mean. And it looks much nicer than satin. Mrs Elsden Smith's little

girl is going to be a bridesmaid too, if the wedding is
in September, she will be the only one because the others
can't get their frocks done in time.

Lots and lots of love
Mary

P.S. Terrific party, not large but good, given tonight
by the Colonel! I hit it off with him he told Daju he was
going to cut him out!

P.P.S. Just had wire from H.Q. saying that Daju is not
to go on either M.T. course, so no Pindi after all! That
means wedding as planned October (provided nothing else
happens). May mean leaving early next year instead of
in May. The firm has just told me that thought they don't
approve of married women in the firm they will keep me on
till the end of this year.

18 Camac Street
Calcutta

30th August 1937

My darling Mummy

Many very happy returns of your birthday! I hope
you had good weather, a happy celebration and lovely
presents! I'm not sending you anything for 3 reasons: I'm
broke after collecting my trousseaux, I don't know what
you want and whatever I send would probably be dutiable
at your end, which makes presents such a problem.
Explain this to Teddy because I'm not sending him one
either. I suggest you give me some idea what you'd like as
combined Christmas and birthday present and I'll bring
it with me when we come on leave next May, if you can bear
waiting all that time! You see, the things could then go
among my personal effects and escape duty. Would you like
linen? You can get sheets, table cloths, etc. Beautifully
worked by a chikon wollah and good material, or another
set of undies like the one we sent last Christmas? or a
carved walnut cigarette box? Or any sort of lacquer work?
Or perhaps you have some secret longing for something I
haven't mentioned – do tell me and I'll do my best. It must
be something really nice because it'll be 2 presents in 1,
also you'll have to wait for it.

I'm writing a letter to Phyllis by ordinary mail
this week, so that there won't be a gap. By the way, I hope
you weren't hurt or offended by what I said in my last
letter, do remember that the cable gave me an awful shock,
because I thought it must mean you were ill or something
awful had happened.

This business with Pamela has got me absolutely beat. I don't know what Daddy is playing at. I do think, though, that he is hiding from Pamela, he's scared stiff of her and her hysterics for which I don't blame him. I hear from Daddy quite often, but his letters are all questions, he tells me very little about himself. Do you know his address? In case you don't and might want it, he is at 23 Womersley Road, London, N. But he will probably be leaving his digs there judging by his comments on the place. I'll let you know his address whenever he changes it. You dill already have my letter containing Richard's comments on the pension business, also what he said about Daddy cutting down your alimony. Don't sit down under that because you don't need to.

I'm glad you managed to get away for a holiday in Eastbourne and hope you had a good time. Rosemary is a good sort, isn't she? I'm hoping Daju will meet her. Have you met Phyllis' precious Molly Hughes, and did you like her? I think she's a pain in the neck, but of course don't breathe a word of that to Phyllis! You should hear what Richard says about her! Thinks she's an utterly empty headed little fool. But the baby's rather sweet. Phyllis' letters have cheered up tremendously since she started working at Imperial airways, it must be a nice job.

Very little news this end, half of Calcutta is down with dengue, the new Colonel has it which is a shame, because he was going to take me to the races last Saturday and of course he couldn't. After all the excitement thinking we were going up to Pindi in about a week's time, things seem very quiet now and lots of time to arrange everything. The firm (in spite of their rule against married women working) have agreed to keep me on till the end of the year, which will help finances. Van Aken said he would keep me on, on his own responsibility which was extraordinarily nice of him because the head office definitely objects. But he is very, very nice also sufficiently important to snap his fingers and the head office over comparatively small thing like that.

Today is practically a holiday in the office. It is their Queen's birthday apparently, so all the men have gone to a terrific lunch party, leaving us with very little work and an enormous chocolate cake for our tea, so that we can celebrate too!

We've been having quite a good time lately but economical because other people have given us the parties!

Lots and lots of love from your very loving daughter
Mary

18 Camac Street
Calcutta

6th September 1937

My darling Mummy,

By the time you get this letter I'll be getting pretty excited!

After the burst of gaiety I told you about in my last letter, things have been very quiet. But we had lunch with Richard yesterday and there was a charming German couple there (we met them at the ladies night) also Leslie and Lynette Chambers. (Phyllis will remember Leslie, I expect). It was very pleasant and we have arranged to see Richard tonight to discuss various matters.

Last night (thank goodness we have Sunday cinemas here) we saw one of the funniest films ever made, if you can follow Scots dialogue! This is "Storm in a tea cup" and is really delightful my ribs are still aching after laughing so much.

Daju and I are going to resign from the 300 club and join the Slap instead. I expect we'll be taken to the 300 sometimes by other people, I'd be sorry not to go there again, but the slap costs just the same and you can get tennis, swimming, etc. there, whereas the 300 is a night club only.

I had such a shock the other day. The first time I had my wedding dress fitted was just after my illness, when I had gone down to 8 stone 2 lbs and it looked lovely. But oh dear! When I tried it on the other day it looked terrible because I have put on 5 lbs! So not I have got to reduce again and Daju is going to teach me squash, which will melt me down to a reasonable weight again pretty quickly.

Elizabeth isn't going to be bridesmaid after all. I am so disappointed. Her mother is coming out but only for a very short while and is going to stay in Simla, so of course Elizabeth is going to stay with her while she is out here. And the times clash, but she and her father have already given us their wedding present - Rs.50/- ! Pretty good present. And the Van Somerens, two pretty red haired girls with charming parents have given us Rs. 40/-. We went to see them yesterday to thank them and discovered they had given it to us so early because they knew they'd be away for the wedding, which is also a great pity. And would you believe it, Richard told us yesterday he was going to be in Darjeeling with the Government from the end of this month onwards and I thought for one awful mement there would be no one to give me away or see the reception! But he is coming down for one day, just for the occasion. We are not going to display our presents, because it would be difficult to arrange for them to be pack up and stored away when we have gone off in the train, also so many of the presents are going to be cheques!

No other news, sorry for a dull letter but this is just to let you know I'm still alive. I warn you, there's sure to be a gap in my letters, because I'll be busy the week before the wedding of course and I will NOT do much letter writing on my honeymoon. Wait till I come back from that, then I'll send you newspaper reports (if any) that Barbara will have cut out and kept for me, also the photos, snaps and full particulars of this stupendous occasion.

Love to all. Love from
Mary

Java Bengal Line
71 Clive Buildings
Calcutta

24th September 1937

My darling Mummy

I've just realised it was mail day yesterday and I'm afraid I completely forgot it! So sorry, I thought I'd better write now because I certainly won't have time next mail day, as it will be only 2 days before the wedding. Just imagine, tomorrow I'll be able to say "in a week's time"!! I would like to send you something personal like a flower from my bouquet, but a flower would be dust by the time it arrived, wouldn't it? I'll send the ribbon it's tied with or something like that.

We had such a hectic party last night. It was Elizabeth Young's farewell party before she goes to Simla. We had already been to a cocktail party at Mrs Eliden-Smith's ("Mrs Smee" she is called, the one who is going to be hostess) and we took Richard with us as he didn't know Mrs Smee and wanted to meet her before the wedding. I enclose an invitation card, nice cards, aren't they? Mrs Smee told me that lots of people had replied that they would be delighted to attend the wedding of her daughter, poor woman, a bit shattering when she's only 30!

Elizabeth had a large party mostly consisting of a regimental team down here for the all India ruggers finals, very nice lads. Fancy playing ruggers in this weather, it's appallingly sticky just now. We had a buffet supper because there were too many of us to go round their dining room table. It was very well done, delicious salads, mushroom pie and lots of hock. We all went on to

Firpos and eventually those who belonged (which included the ruggers team) went to 300 club a very merry party, which broke up at 3 am! Oh, dear I am sleepy now.

27th September.

My last week of freedom begun! There was a letter from Auntie May last mail. I've send the Underhills a card also Thets and one to the Bracken. Please explain to Aunts Bar, Bee, Winnie, etc. that I couldn't send any to them because I didn't know their addresses, anyway they didn't write to me.

We went to see Michael Cleery, Chubby Chapman and Reggie Haddow the other day. Phyllis will remember them. Does she remember his Irish terrier bitch, called Biddy? Because Michael is going home next year and we are going to adopt Biddy, she's a delightful animal. We may also buy their wireless. It's a very good one and they won't want it because the chummery is breaking up.

Daju's Indian storekeeper is going to give ma an Indian silver powder box! I'm so thrilled it sounds lovely. He is giving this to me because regulations don't allow him to give Daju anything. We have been given a beautiful pale blue tablecloth with white flowers on it by Mrs Howard, the manageress of the Y.W There's forgiveness for you after the dance I led that poor women!

We have also adopted a ginger kitten, an adorable thing known by Daju as Bisum (Arabic for cat) by myself as Esme, and by everyone else as ginger Joe. So with Biddy, buttons and bisum we are starting off with a menagerie!

Give my love to everyone and explain this letter is, of course to the whole family.

Much love from

Mary

11 Camac Street
Calcutta

17th October 1937

My darling Mummy,

Your letter to me on my birthday was waiting for
me when we returned from our honeymoon. Thank you for
all your good wishes for me, they seem to be coming true
because I am very happy, and Harry is too. He is looking
much better, has got very brown and has put on weight.
That applies to me too! Chandipore is on the sea so we
bathed every day, wandered about in shorts, played gold
on the sands, fished, with a mosquito net!!, went to bed
early and ate enormously! It was just like being a kid
again!

There are only five bungalows at Chandipore, it is
not a popular resort but a place where experiments are
carried out with ammunition, shells, etc. There is a big
gun. Only military people are allowed there. The sea ebbs
2 miles out, 2 miles of flat sands which reached out on
either side as far as you could see! The coast was flat and
grassy and the bungalows are prettily set in clusters of
what looks like scotch firs. There is a line of mountains
just visible in the back ground, the sunsets were
magnificent and all reflected on the sands, altogether a
lovely place, most romantic! Harry's dog Buttons adores
the sea, so we all had fun his dog is a black mongrel that
looks like a Labrador.

About the wedding cake, we left a list of addresses
with Flewy & Irinca who made the cake, but when we came
back we found they had sent you a small piece only, so we

told them to send you more. We also found they sent out all the pieces from "Mr & Mrs Parker" because the bill was sent to Richard, so they thought it was his wedding!

The photos aren't ready yet but we have seen the proofs, and I know you will be pleased with them. The only thing that spoils the group is that Richard is looking very grim! I don't know why he obviously enjoyed the reception.

Oh mummy darling, if only you could have been there. You would have simply loved it, everyone was so merry and friendly all the uniforms looked so smart. It somehow seemed like an informal party, everyone mixed so well and I think I had a chat with every person in the room, including some Indian officers, who were terribly flattered apparently, and I was told that I was an unusually jolly bride! It was such fun. As for Harry, he went round kissing all the girls, you should have seen the expression on my bosses faces (3 Dutch men from the office came) when they saw him!

I'll tell you all about the presents in my next letter, but I'm busy now writing "thank you" letters for them. Thetis comment when I wrote to her was that thoist of every variety had been well catered for quite true too. We had 3 cocktail shakers, but we heard of an unfortunate couple who were given 14! a popular present just now.

We have a big room with the bedroom part curtained off and a large bathroom, where we have managed to store most of our boxes, but even so our chief problem is where to put our boxes. Harry has to have the awful long ones for swords. This is an annexe of the place I stayed at before the wedding so we get the same food, the good quality of this being the chief reason for wanting to stay at the same place. So it doesn't matter if you forget and address your letters to no. 18, because it's all under the same management.

I notice you didn't get my letter about the pension. I asked Richard about it ages ago and I'm afraid this isn't good news. This pension is a kind of insurance business Daddy has to pay into it, but when you cease to be his wife it doesn't matter whether by death or divorce, he can't pay into it any more, the whole thing just lapses. If he marries again he can, if he wants to start a new series of payments for his new wife. If Daddy did that Pamela will get a pension he probably didn't knowing Daddy! So she will not have a pension. But in either case I'm afraid you don't get one. That at any rate is what Richard thinks but he advises you to apply to the India office to make sure, he won't guarantee that his is right and I hope he isn't.

Please explain to all relations that much as we wanted to send them wedding cake, the supply ran out, because people ate so much of it at the reception, I don't blame them, it was a damn good cake.

My love to the family, lots of love from
Mary Cuerden!

The next page is the only remaining page
of a letter my mother wrote, describing
their wedding and reception. I have included
it purely for the cartoon sketch explaining
who is who in a group photograph,
annoyingly missing. It well illustrates
her irrepressible sense of humour.
I obviously have no idea when she wrote it,
so I have included it after the letter she
wrote when she returned from her honeymoon
as I doubt she would have written it while
on honeymoon! In any case, she wouldn't have
had the photos until some time after the
wedding, which took place on 2nd October, 1937.

CALCUTTA.

- 5 -

we decided was the only place to give us a dinner worthy of our
appetite.   Their crab and asparagus soup is a dream - a damned
solid dream, almost a meal in itself - then we had fried rice,
mixed up with prawns and other oddments, chicken chow-chow,
stewed chicken with mushrooms, slices of pineapple and beans,
also a kind of omelette with prawns and mushrooms in it and
shredded ham over it!   And finished up with lichees and cream!

Lots of love, and keep cheerful,

Mary

P.S.   Have the photos arrived yet, and
if so, don't you think they're
good?   Here is a rough diagram
to explain who's who in the group: —

Capt Macfarlane
best man

Harry'thump
poor thing

Richard
(not dracula as
you might think)
"Cupid"
(Rick Colquhoun; so-called
because he
introduced us)

Mrs Elsden-Smith
hostess

Eileen Keegan

Barbara
Keegan

The Bride
(isn't she lovely?)

little
Sally Jewson

11 Camac Street
Calcutta

1st November 1937

My darling Mummy,

Thank you for your letter. You are quite right
I do feel quite an old married woman by now, tomorrow
is a month from the wedding! I'm sure I can tell you he
is happy too. I am very happy mummy darling, Harry is a
wonderful person you can talk to him about anything, he
so understands and always has something sensible and
comforting to say in any difficulty. Last night we lay
in bed and talked half the night about religion (we had
hardly discussed it at all before) and his ideas were
really beautiful, and so broad minded at the same time.
I know you will love him, for himself not just for my
sake. He admires you tremendously for your courage and
entirely agreed with me when I said it was an enduring
courage because you've needed it for a long, long time,
and it hasn't failed you.

Harry has been ill during the last week with
slight fever, the doctor didn't say whether it was a
recurrence of his malaria or a go of dengue, but it was
very mild anyway, and as his C.O. Major Windle has just
returned from leave Harry was able to leave things to him
and go to bed, before the wedding when Major Windle was
away, Harry had to carry on whether he was ill or not! He
was allowed out for the first time yesterday.

I'm glad you celebrated on the wedding day, did you
get tight on sherry! Now I want to tell you all about the
wedding because the account of it in my last letter was
rather sketchy.

For two nights before the wedding I stayed with
Mr & Mrs Elsden Smith (she was the good lady who wrote
to you, and took the part of hostess at the reception).
Well, the morning of the wedding I spent my time at the
hairdresser's and having my facial. Eileen Keegan, one
of the bridesmaids, goes in for beauty treatment, so gave
me the face massage, very soothing to the nerves. Miss
Anna, the Italian hairdresser seemed almost as thrilled
as I was and she did my hair in a new special way, soft,
loose sausage curls all the way round my head, coming
up quite high on my forehead to form a soft frame for my
face. It was certainly very pretty but too difficult to
keep in order for any except special occasions. Lunch
was at one, cold chicken and sweet corn (lovely) and fruit
salad, I wasn't hungry! Then the bouquets arrived from
the florists, mine consisted of cream roses and clematis
and ferns. Mrs E Smith's was red roses and green fern
stuff, but the wretched Indian florists sent puce roses
with scarlet ribbons, and the same for the bridesmaids,
and it was too late to do anything about it! Then I rested
for half an hour, then bathed, dressed and was all ready
when Richard called for me at 3. So we went down into
the garden and the Smees (Elden Smiths nickname) took
snaps of us (haven't got the prints from the Smees yet).
The Smees set off for the church first, Richard and I
following about five minutes later. We were punctual
absolutely on the tick of 3.30. The bridesmaids were
waiting for me at the entrance, Sally was told how to hold
my veil, they queued up behind me and off we set up the
aisle. When I reached Harry he was looking so stern that
I felt panicky and thought he was wishing himself out
of it! I felt so dithery that I blindly thrust my bouquet
at Richard and knelt down and shook so much that Harry

found it quite difficult to get the ring on my finger. He was quite calm, in fact, while they were waiting for me the Colonel exclaimed "good god, the man's blasé!" And that was why he looked stern because he was trying not to laugh. It didn't last long, then we all seemed to be in the vestry quite suddenly me and Harry and Barbara and Eileen and Sally and Richard and Mac (the best man) and everybody was kissing everybody and little Sally looked so sweet she nearly got eaten! And then down the aisle as Mrs Cuerden, Harry wearing a broad grin by now and as for me, if it hadn't been for my long veil, I'd have danced down to the strains of something that sounded like a funeral march being played by the organ. "Here comes the bride" was played when I came in, then through the arch of swords (eleven on each side) and masses of confetti and press photographers. And off in the car between lines of Harry's men all cheering. (They'd arranged that between themselves which pleased Harry immensely). Arrived at the US Club, went upstairs, Phyllis will know the room, and there at the end was a huge three tiered cake on a table and on the floor by the table the most immense basket of roses I've ever seen "From the JBL and the KLM" the office! People soon began to roll up and we had to stand by the door and shake hands, and didn't we just feel sorry for the Royal family by the time we'd shaken hands with over 80 guests! Then downstairs again and out onto the lawn for the wedding group, etc. to be taken. If they're ready in time, I'll send them by this mail but don't be disappointed if I don't because with Harry being in bed for the last week and me working, it's been difficult to get things done. While the photographs were being taken people came out onto the verandah and tantalised us by drinking tad and eating sandwiches. When we went back the tea was

finished and the champagne had just begun to circulate.
(I might say here that I had very little and Harry had
much too much, he kept stealing mine). The cake was cut,
health's were drunk and the speeches began. Richard's
was very short and nothing worth remembering, Harry was
heckled shamefully but wasn't worth listening too anyway,
he started off by saying he hoped none of the guests felt
as uncomfortable as he did, cried of "shame!", and Richard
said I ought to smack him. When Harry had petered out,
Mac got up to say "I've just been told to thank you for the
bridesmaids, and I thought for one delirious moment that
the bridesmaids had been given to him!" and so on, far the
best speech. Then the thing became a party, Harry went
found kissing all the girls so I retaliated by kissing all
the men I liked, the Dutchmen's eyes were popping! Three
of them came and seemed to think it all most peculiar!

We stayed at the club till about 5.45, we had to
leave to change and get to the station. We arrived only
just in time. The train journey took four hours then we
had a 16 mile drive in a lorry from the station to the
bungalow. Luckily we managed to sleep in the train a bit,
or we'd have been absolutely whacked.

Please thank Phyllis for her letter and tell Angela
Harry was delighted with Angela's, which I showed to him,
and is going to write to her some time. Poor Harry, Daddy
is annoyed because he hasn't written to him and he just
doesn't know what to write to Daddy! Writing to you was
different, he said.

And will everyone please not be annoyed because
I've only written to you this week, but it's very long this
letter and meant for everyone because you'll all want to

read a detailed account of the wedding, also I must write to various aunts who've written to me.

Much love to all, your very loving daughter
Mary

P.S. Sorry about the photographs! We'll send them next week for certain.

11 Camac Street
Calcutta

14th December 1937

My darling Mummy,

This is to wish you a very merry Christmas and the
best possible luck for the New Year. So glad to hear you've
adopted a black cat, I hope it does its job as a mascot! Give
it a kiss from me. How nice to have a cat again.

And now I hope you won't be disappointed at my
next bit of news. Harry and I have decided that it would
be best not to send home my present for you, because of
this wretched duty business. It would double the cost
of the things, I find. So they'll come with us among our
things next year. I'll tell you about them anyway. I've
got a tablecloth for you, not a huge thing but something
for a tea table you know, rather nicely worked and some
ridiculous little squares to match, meant to be table
napkins. I got this because I remembered innumerable
occasions when we looked at cloths and mourned over
stains. If you like the idea I'll get some more, they're not
expensive out here, if you think it's a dull present let me
know what you would like and I'll bring back something
to offset the dull usefulness of that. But really truly, I'm
sure you'll like it, it is a pretty piece of work.

What a pity you have to try and let the house. You
will miss the garden so terribly. Without wishing to be
a wet blanket it's rather a hopeless effort, isn't it? I
remember so many empty houses in Egmont Road.

The actual number of presents received jointly was
42 (so far: one or two to come) and I personally received 2,

my two were a complete set of undies from Mrs Elsden Smith made by her chikon wollah (with a very naughty nightie), and a silver powder box from an Indian woman whom I have never seen. Her husband wanted to give a wedding present but rules and regulations were against it, he is one of Harry's men.

The 42 consist of: Cheques (including yours and Daddy's) 9 wedding reception, 1 cocktail set, 1 cocktail shakers, 2 chota hazri sets, 2 soup bowls, spoons, etc. (Chinese), 1 set condiments, 1 set liquer glasses, 1 lemonade set, 1 assorted glasses, 1 grapefruit glasses, 1 set ashtrays, 2 book ends, 2 pairs, clocks (including 1 electric) 3 silver cigarette box, 1 bed spread, 1 pair of duchesse sets, doyleys, etc. 3 sets salad bowl, 1 set beer mugs, 1 Stuart crystal vase, 1 finger bowl, 1 set silk carpet, 1 table lamp with shade (camel bladder) 1 standard lamp and table lamp to match, with shades, 1 pair of cushions.

I think that's all, but I've written this all out from memory in the office.

It's a perfect scream about the Underhills.

I've lost Auntie Bar's address. Please, please sent it by the very next mail or she'll be so offended if I don't answer her letter.

We're going to a cocktail party tonight, followed by a "soup and sausage" supper. This is with some people called Mundy, we met Mrs Munday at the Elsden Smith's the other evening, and she seemed to take a fancy to us. Isn't it lovely the way people out here throw out invitations the first time they meet you? So friendly, if only people at home were like that!

With best love from

Mary

J. B. L.
CALCUTTA.

11, Camac Street,

CALCUTTA.

17th January, 1938.

My darling Mummy,

It's a shocking long time since I last wrote - three
weeks, I believe. Christmas weeks, you understand. We had a
pretty hectic Christmas, but unfortunately developed appalling
colds, which are only just getting better.

We had a grand time when the Navy was in, because
although my old friends on the "Norfolk" were no longer on board,
Harry met an old school friend on the "Indus", and we palled up
with the crowd on that ship no end, they kept asking us to dinner
on board, and cocktail parties and so on. We gave a Monopoly
party for them, which was a great success; they got so fascinated
by the game, that they refused to have drinks, they didn't want to
interrupt the game! We also made friends with the "Hindustan"
and the "Emerald", in fact the only ship we didn't have friends oh
was the "Norfolk", which made itself very unpopular this year, by
the general unfriendliness of the new crowd on board. The "Indus"
and the "Hindustan" hope to be in Bombay the same time we are, when
we go over to catch our ship, and we have been practically commanded
to call and see them. So we are going to Bombay a day earlier, in
order to have one whole day there, and the hope Naval hospitality
won't make us miss our ship!

The Viceroy's and Governor's Balls were much the same as

J. B. L.
CALCUTTA.

- 2 -

last year, gorgeous as spectacles, wonderful frocks and uniforms,
but oh dear! from a dancing point of view, just the most awful
scrum!

I suppose you have met Eric by how.   What to you think
of him?   Shy, but very nice, don't you think?   He writes really
brilliant letters, they are better than his conversation.

Well, this is my last month at the office, and I am not
altogether sorry.   There is a new man in the office, whom I do
not like.   Also it is difficult sometimes, when I am asked to play
tennis in the afternoon.

I had to see an eye-specialist the other day, luckily there
is a military one which means I saw him free being a military wife,
but the new glasses cost ℞.15/-, which was tiresome.   Apparently I
had outgrown the old glasses, and they were making matters worse.
And Harry has had trouble with his teeth, so we have been a sorry
couple!   He went to the dentish before Christmas and was told that
he must have three teeth out at once, or he'd have a poisoned face,
but he insisted on waiting till after Christmas, and sure enough his
face swelled up.   But when he went to have them out, they discovered
it w as only one that was giving the trouble, so he only had to have
one out after all.   I must say he kept extraordinarily bright and
cheerful all the time, though it must have been most unpleasant for
him, most people would have been creeping miseries.

101

J. B. L.
CALCUTTA.

- 3 -

20th Jan.

Went to see Richard last night, and he said he'd just had a letter from Eric, on whom you have apparently made a terrific impression, quite cut me out, in fact! Richard said he simply adored you.

I asked Richard about this business of Daddy demanding china, books, etc., and Richard said there was no obligation whatever for you to give them to him. Of course, an arrangement should have been made legally at the time of the divorce about furniture to belong to you, and so on, but according to the law, a man cannot demand property back (even if it really did belong to him originally) after it has been in the possession of someone else for six years. Well, you've had all that stuff for over six years, haven't you? So Daddy has no legal claim to it. I thought you would be relieved to hear that; it must have been so appallingly worrying, wondering how much more Daddy was going to demand!

Richard's wife is such a dear. Nothing to look at, and has to wear those horrid contraptions on her legs, like Maurice used to wear, but so cheerful and sensible. And Richard is so obviously devoted to her, they are charming together.

Well, I'll soon be a lady of leisure. It will seem strange. At the present moment the entire office is very worked up about Princess Juliana's baby; we do wish it would buck up and arrive, because we'll get a holiday, and if it's a

J. B. L.
CALCUTTA.

- 4 -

boy, probably two days' holiday!   And all the Dutch community
will get together and celebrate.

This evening we are going to see "Victoria the Breat".
I wonder if you've seen it yet.

My love to everyone.

Your very loving daughter,

Mary

11, Camac Street,
Calcutta.
31st Jan. 1938.

My darling Mummy,
　　　　I'm afraid I missed the last mail, though I meant to write, because I had to be inoculated, and my arm was too stiff to write. I couldn't type either, I just supervised the other girl's work at the office! Harry and I were both done, because there was a typhoid scare among the European population, and several deaths.

　　　　Harry and I are delighted with the present, which we got yesterday from a girl Eric met on board. As she was coming to Calcutta, he entrusted it to her. It's simply lovely, so original, and a delicious scent. Harry sends his thanks for his portion of it.

　　　　Last Saturday we dined with Richard and Mary, an had a remarkably amusing evening, though we didn't do anything, just sat and talked. Richard paid Harry a ve great compliment, because when we return from leave he wants Harry as a Military Intelligence Officer to work und him; he thinks Harry has far more intelligence than the present man, who is considerably senior! It would me more pay, not much, but still! But he is most emphatic that we are not to bank on it, as Harry's Corp is short of officers, and may well refuse to let him go But wouldn't it be lovely for Harry and Richard to work together?

　　　　I got permission from one of the Dutchmen in the office to bring a friend out to Dum-Dum one day to ha a look at the K.L.M. planes, and have asked Mary.

2.

She was very pleased, chiefly because of I thought of her,
I believe. We plan to go next Wednesday, when I am a
lady of leisure!

Can you believe it, we leave Calcutta in six weeks'
time and sail on 19th March (touch wood) on the "Ranchi"!
Isn't it incredible? I wonder if you'll recognise Harry
from his photos? You won't know me, I weigh a stone
less than when you last saw me, and my hair's done a
different way! I'll know you all - except perhaps
Angela, I'm told she's grown enormous, and looks more
like 15 than 11! Tell her she'd better stop growing if
she's taller than Harry he'll spank her!

3rd Feb.

lady of leisure now - bit bored by it.

Juliana had her baby, and we were asked to the
celebrations - was that a party! We started at the 300
Club with champagne at 7 o'clock, and didn't get home
till 1! When the Dutch celebrate they go all out.
Harry was the only Englishman in the party; there were
about 4 English girls. We didn't feel the least bit
out of it, though, everyone was so friendly, and
introduced themselves, German fashion. They had a
marvellous cold supper, after which we danced, stopping
every now and then to sing Dutch songs, and some
English ones, and there were a few speeches - in Dutch,
but translated for our benefit. Then we went on to the
Casanova - a huge party of us, all very merry, and
after that most of them went on to some other club, but
I firmly took Harry home, he was far from sober
and had to drive at about 10 m.p.h. He had such
a head the next day! Wasn't too bright myself.

3

After all, it was free champagne. They also insisted on us trying their special Dutch gin, which was foul. There was a dear old professor there, with a straggly grey beard, who could speak about 17 languages. He was a dear.

Yesterday Mary Parker, her companion Sheila Sandilands, and I, drove out to Dum Dum to see the K.L.M. plane. I 'phoned up the aerodrome and was told it was due in at 12, but when we arrived there was no sign of Mr. de Jong or the plane, so I went to the office and was told they had just got a message that it had developed engine trouble and gone back to Allahabad, and would be in Calcutta at 6 that evening! So we just had to go back, it was disappointing. I was especially fed up, because I had arranged it all to amuse Mary, who was really quite thrilled about it. She was very sporting and quite realised of course I couldn't help it, still it was a pity.

This letter is for everyone, of course, with best love from Harry and me.

We are so very glad to hear you are seriously thinking about coming out to India again — and are looking forward to talking it over!

Your very loving daughter
Mary.

11, Camac Street,
Calcutta.
1st March 1938.

My darling Mummy,

Just look at the date! Not three weeks to go — we sail on the 19th from Bombay on the "Ranchi." I am telling you this again, because Phyllis' letter (which arrived by the first All-Up Mail) asks the name of the boat, etc, so you must have forgotten, or else didn't get that particular letter. We are not flying from Marseilles after all, as it doesn't really save enough time to justify the extra expense, although we wanted every moment that we could manage in England. We are coming overland from Marseilles. I think we arrive in England about the 4th or 5th April. But you could find out from your end.

I'm glad Phyllis' dance was such a success — give her my congrats., and thanks for her letter. Were you able to go and see the show? The newspaper was rather scathing about it. Sorry about Phyllis being unwell. That is the drawback to office-work, it makes you tired without giving you any exercise, and you feel disinclined for exercise when you come to the end of a working day. It would be well worth her while to get up ten minutes earlier and do some really energetic exercises. She used to be keen on skipping, why doesn't she do ten minutes skipping in the garden before breakfast? It would jog her liver up no end.

I'm a grass widow! Harry went out to camp on Sunday night, and will return on Wednesday evening. He has gone about 25 miles out of Calcutta. I sleep and have breakfast in the flat upstairs, with a rather charming couple by the name of Preeston. Harry is coming in this evening to a cocktail party the Preestons are giving; we'll just have a bite of dinner together, then off he'll have to go again. It's not so bad really, because I dined with Richard and Mary last night, I shall lunch with them to-day, and lots of people have said I can pop in on them for tea if I'm lonely, so what with one thing and another, the days pass. Last night was great fun, it wasn't a party, just dinner en famille (if that's how you spell it) and afterwards we turned out the lights and told ghost stories. Richard made up some perfectly <u>horrible</u> ones.

I'm taking advantage of Harry's absence to do a spot of turning out, and sorting out what we are taking home and what we are storing. What a business!

Harry, you will be glad to hear, is much better, and his boils have all gone. The X-ray of his jaw showed nothing, so the dentist says the boils must have been just the rest of the poison working its way out after the poisoned tooth was extracted. Four days in the open will probably do him a lot of good, too.

On Sunday we spent the day at the Angus Jute Mills with the Procters. I have mentioned them before, the mills are about 30 miles up the river. They have their own swimming-pool, filled with fresh well water, and we had the first bathe of the year, which was very welcome as it has suddenly turned very hot — about 88° in the shade — just think of that, Phyllis' letter told me you have had snow! I actually did some diving for the first time in my life! We meant to return to Calcutta after tea, as Harry had to drop me and then go out to camp, but they said they had killed a pet goose for dinner specially

3

for our benefit, so what could we do but stay? We didn't get back to Calcutta till about 11. Anyway, the goose was very nice, and it really was a lovely day, we went to the Club they have there, and played deck tennis and ping-pong, so what with swimming and everything it was pretty energetic.

I suppose you will get this letter before the one I wrote to P. last week, as that was ordinary mail, and this will go by the first of the All-up mails from India. Isn't it marvellous to be able to get in touch with each other in a week, without the former expense of airmail? Really it is an amazing scheme.

With very much love to you all from Harry
and from
Your loving daughter
Mary.

ss. Modasa.

1st Feb. 1989.

My dear Mummy,

What a trip! Bitterly, biting cold - couldn't get warm in bed even, though 1 got the Stewardess to give me an extra blanket and a hot, water-bottle. To-day we are in the Bay, and she is rolling quite a bit, but it's a good deal warmer.

2.

Last night the women had a conference and decided not to change for dinner because it was too cold.

The crowd on board is too dreadful for words. Do you remember the rough-looking men? There are fifty of them, bound for Port Said to join the Palestine Police Force.

The first day, I unpacked as soon as the car had disappeared round the corner, and that kept me busy till Tea. At tea I sat next to a middle-aged woman, and got into conversation with her. She is

3.

rather nice; it is her first trip and she is continually getting lost. Now she comes to me and gets me to take her to her cabin, she simply can't find it by herself! She is on her way to Madras to visit her married daughter, whose husband is in the I.C.S. Her name is Mrs. Hodgson

I am at the Chief Engineer's table. The C.E. on one side and Mrs. Hodgson on the other. Opposite me the Chief Steward has unkindly placed two old buffers who tuck their napkins into their waistcoats and eat cheese with their knives, swallowing about half the knife

4.

in the process. One of them isn't a bad old sort, he and I are going to run the tote together on the ship's daily run. That was my idea. I honestly believe I'm the only person on board with any ideas or the capacity for carrying them out. Yesterday I organised a vingt-et-un party between tea and supper. It was too cold to venture out on deck, so indoor amusement was badly needed. It wasn't my fault that only three elderly ladies (including Mrs. Hodgson) could be persuaded to play.

5.

There is a loquacious lady by the name of Mrs. Brookes who affords me constant though secret amusement, chiefly because she always refers to the younger of her two small sons as "the wee fellow", to his huge and obvious discomfort.

She is getting off at Malta, and so are a lot of others. By the time we have disembarked the fifty "toughs" at Port Said,

6.

there will be only 28 passengers
left !! I don't think Snow - White
will have much competition — quite
possibly I won't even have the
chance to wear it.

<u>3ʳᵈ Feb.</u>

There is to be no dancing till
we have disembarked the fifty "tonghs"
at Port Said, as it would be
difficult to prevent them joining in,
and they are not considered
suitable — which is true enough!

7.

And after Port Said, I don't think there will be enough people left to make dancing worth while! So we are in for a lively time!

She is rolling a good deal now and we have got those funny things on the tables to prevent the plates sliding about. But it isn't really rough, it's just a long steady roll. It's getting warmer.

I'm sorry this is such a dull letter, but honestly there is just nothing to write about. On the "Mulbera" the ship's officers used to join in and help to make fun, but the Chief Engineer told me that on this ship the Captain is frightfully strict

8.

and the officers are not allowed even to have a drink with passengers, let alone dance or help with the games.

I spend the time reading or knitting, with an occasional game of whist or vingt-et-un. Now that it is warmer, this is varied by a walk round the deck with Mrs. Hodgson — or by myself. The "toughs" monopolize the ping-pong and quoits. They are such a rough noisy horrible crowd that nobody even tries to get a turn at these games.

Well, after Port Said things should be better.

Much love to you all,
Mary.

S.S. Modasa

7th Feb. 1959

Dear Flip,

You and Mummy had better swop letters because you'll have completely different versions! The first three days were really too dreadful for words. Then things cheered up.

There are some young naval and marine officers on board, and on Saturday they suddenly decided to get up a concert, to take place the same night! I was asked to take part in a sketch, and was the only girl in the show! The

2.

"toughs" — the men for the Palestine Police
Force — sang, played on the mouth-organ,
and also did one or two short sketches.
It wasn't a patch on the "Mulbera"
affair, but not bad considering the
extremely short notice!

There is a remarkably pretty girl
on board called Mrs. Shone, whose
husband is in the I.M.S., who is going
as far as Madras. She is great fun,
and we play games a lot together.
The night after the concert she and I
each picked a team (nine a side) and
got a neutral person to choose words
and put them to us — a spelling bee
on B.B.C. lines. We borrowed the
dinner gong to gong the mistakes. It
was surprisingly funny — one enterprising man spelt "meringue"

MOURRANG !!!   The next day (yesterday) Mrs. Shone and I borrowed a dictionary and a typewriter and prepared two competitions, which duly took place last night amidst great hilarity. One was another spelling-bee, and the other was a competition for saying 'tongue-twisters.' Here are three of the 16 tongue-twisters that we put to the unfortunate competitors:-

1) The Leith police condoneth and dismisseth us.

2) Are you copper-bottoming them, my man? No, I'm aluminiuming them, mum.

3) A cap, a cock, a kettle from Popocatapetl

The last is mere gibberish but maddeningly difficult. The twisters had to be said 3 times quickly.

The deck tennis is now in full swing, and to-day has been distinctly

4

warmer — but I am still wearing my thick jumper.

To-morrow we reach Malta, but don't know yet at what time. It's rather a pity, but all the young naval and marine lads, and some other pleasant people, are getting off at Malta.

To-night being their last night on board they are planning a surprise, but I'll have to tell you about that in my Port Said letter, as letters for Malta have to be posted to-night.

I wonder how you're all getting along, and if you have had your tonsils out yet?

Lots of love,
from
Mary.

S.S. Madara

11ᵗʰ Feb. 1939.

My dear Phyllis,

I believe I finished my last letter by telling you the Marines were planning a surprise for their last evening on board. Well, two of them and Mrs. Shone, acted the titles of well-known books and plays, and the rest of us had to guess. Most of them were quite clever, but not specially funny; the really good effort was kept till the end, when they held up a pair of trousers and showed us a hole in the seat. What famous book did

2.

that represent? — "Gone With the Wind"!! After that the party broke up in some disorder and some of us went off and played newmarket.

When we reached Malta these lads had to go off and join their various ships, but we met two of them for tea, and after trying to find some form of amusement (having a vague idea that there must be places of historical interest, but not knowing what or where they were) we went to the cinema and saw an ancient Jack Buchanan film. They came back to the ship for a last drink, but the "toughs" were wandering about in all stages of drunkenness, and the Chief Officer

3.

advised us to keep well out of their way, so we saw the two Marine lads off and retired to our respective cabins and locked the door.

Since then nothing has happened at all! They have put up the swimming pool, but have not yet filled it.

There is one nice man left on board (the others are all dreadful), who is generally called "Statesman" because he is on his way to Calcutta to work as a reporter on the "Statesman". He and I and Mrs. Stone play three-handed bridge in the evenings. During the day, I read and knit and play singles at deck tennis with Mrs S. (Statesman has hurt his leg and

4

can't play games) Occasionally we vary that with ping-pong.

As you can see it is one ceaseless round of hectic gaiety, and I don't know how I'll stand the strain.

Tomorrow (Sunday) we reach Port Said. It will be grand to get some letters -- and get rid off this toughs!

I hope my next letter will be a little more interesting!

My love to all the family.

Your affectionate sister,

Mary.

The Metropole Hotel
Rawalpindi.
11th March 1939.

My dear Mummy,

That cable must have been a surprise!
Everything's happened so suddenly, I really
don't know whether I'm on my head or heels!

The ship spent two days in Madras, and
Helen Shone asked me and Statesman to lunch
with her on the second day. While we were at
her flat, the local B.I. agents rang up and
asked to speak to me, and told me they had
had a 'phone message from my husband in
Calcutta, who wanted me to leave the ship and
catch the next train to Calcutta. Five minutes
later who should ring up but Harold Lawson!!
(Phyllis will remember him, a long streak of a man
who lived at the boarding house in Russell Street).
Well, he had been transferred by his firm
from Calcutta to Madras, so Harry had got
in touch with him and told him to look after
me. He told me that Harry's leave of

126

2.

one month had been cancelled, but he had been allowed ten days to meet me. When Harry reached Calcutta he found the ship was going to be late, in the usual B.I. fashion, and if I wanted to see anything of him, I must catch the train, which would arrive in Calcutta two days before the ship.

Helen insisted that we should have our lunch with her, then Statesman and I dashed back to the ship, and Statesman packed like a hero while I dashed round doling out tips and telling the 4th officer to hand over my heavy baggage to Cox & Kings in Calcutta, and saying goodbyes. Then Harold Lawson came on board and took me in his car to Binny's, the B.I. agents, who made a reservation on the train for me, and rang up Harry. But the line was so bad I couldn't hear a word. Back to the ship, where the steward had specially arranged an early dinner for me, and on to the station. Helen and her husband, Statesman and Harold came to see me off, and loaded me with chocolates and magazines.

3.

I had a compartment to myself in the train, and it seemed a very long and tedious journey – two nights and a day. The train got into Howrah at 10 a.m on Sunday morning, and of course Harry was there to meet me. Some friends of ours called Measor had placed their flat at our disposal for the morning, so we went there and I had a much-needed bath, while Harry told me that he had arranged for me to stay at a hotel in Pindi, as Calcutta was really much too far to visit on ten days' leave, and apparently it is difficult to get longer leave, although he is supposed to to get three months' leave a year from the frontier!

We spent the rest of the day dashing round Calcutta trying to see people, but nearly everyone was out. Then we drove out to the Angus Mills, as we were spending the night with the Procters. We spent the rest day at the Mills. Buttons was looking remarkably well, but didn't remember us

4.

at first, but after a bit he got very excited,
and obviously began to realise who we were.
In the evening we went into Calcutta with Bill
and Janet and had dinner at Firpos. There was
no one there that we knew so after a few
dances we went on to the 300 Club. There
again the crowd was very different, though we
saw some old friends. But we left early, as
Bill had to be up at five the next morning.
The next day we bade Janet and Bill farewell,
collected Buttons and thanked the Braids for
looking after him so well, and drove into
Calcutta, where we spent a busy day visiting
the Bank, Cox & King's, etc. I also popped
into my old office, where they all seemed very
pleased to see me, even the bearers remembered
me! Then we discovered the "Modasa" was
due in at six, so we would have plenty
of time to see it before catching our train,
so we dashed down, and were enthusiastically
greeted by the Chief, the doctor and Statesman.
Of course Harry really wanted to find out

5.

whether I'd been a good girl on board or not! But all he heard was that I had enlivened an otherwise dull voyage, by putting sardines in the net that was put out to catch flying-fish, painting the doctor's fingernails with red varnish when I caught him asleep in a deck chair, and similar pleasantries. Helen, of course, was my partner in all these crimes. Statesman came to see us off in the train.

We arrived in Delhi the following night, and were told that as our train was an hour late we had missed our connection to Pindi, and there wouldn't be another till 7 in the morning. There was nothing for it but to stay the night at a hotel, so we went along to the Grand Hotel, and 'phoned Eric from there. He had just returned from a dinner party (it was about half-past ten) and he came dashing round. He is looking extremely well, and is much more cheerful, and more human! Harry, who had always loathed him before, changed his mind about him.

6.

We were up early the next morning to catch our train, and after another long and dusty day (but thank goodness it was cool) we arrived at Pindi at 4 the following _morning_! It wasn't any use going to the hotel at that hour, so we slept on benches, in the waiting-room till 7, then went on to the hotel where we both had much needed baths and a large breakfast. Harry had to catch another train that evening to Manzai, where he joined the convoy to Wana. In the meantime he took me to see two married couples here he knew, who promised to look after me, and arranged for me to join the club. He had to leave directly after dinner. I went to bed early and had the first real sleep I'd had since leaving the ship, and feeling slightly more human this morning.

Harry has got me a lovely little wireless set, and left Buttons with me. When I have got the ~~wireles~~ aerial fixed

7.

up, I imagine my chief amusements will be listening to the wireless and taking Buttons for walks. I think Pindi's a beastly place, it has no Maidan, no European shops, and it's horribly old. I have had to dig out my old tweed costume again.

Do you know, I haven't had a single letter from any of you since I left! I had a letter from Mike at Port Said, but it was written from Ireland and gave me no news about you! I am sure you <u>must</u> have written, so I am hoping the letters will be sent on here through the agency of Cox's. Please write to me here quickly, though, I want to know what's happened to you all!

I really couldn't write this out all over again, so you must consider this letter is for all of you.

Much love to you all,
from

your loving daughter, Mary.

Metropole Hotel,
Rawalpindi.

2nd April 1939.

My dear Flip,

Thanks for your letter. Glad you are having a rather cheerier time. When is Dick going to come to the boil?

This week has been pretty hectic. It was Pindi Week, and something had been arranged for every afternoon, polo, races, horse-shows, etc., but unfortunately it thundered and rained — and rained like blazes, so everything had to be cancelled till yesterday, which was a simply glorious day, like summer at its best in England — not too hot — so the races were on after all.

I went to the races with a certain Major Geoffs, a middle-aged bachelor,

2.

rather good looking, and very pleasant company. I won Rs. 45/- on the first race, but lost on all the others, however I was Rs. 15/- up at the end — and quite content with that. I wonder if you remember — or if I ever showed you — a white frock I got at a guinea shop in town? It was very plain with pleats down to the front to the waist and red buttons and belt. It also had a coatee with short sleeves and a red and blue scarf attached. Anyway, that's what I wore, with my white halo hat and blue-and-white prom. shoes, blue-and-white bag and white gloves, and by Jove it did look smart — everyone was staring, various boy-friends told me I looked utterly marvellous, and Geoffs told me it was obvious I bought my clothes in Paris !!! I kept very quiet about guinea gown shops!

3.

I got photographed several times by the local & press, and if any of them turn out well, needless to say you shall see the result.

On Wednesday some strange young man floated in and introduced himself as Capt. Forster (John) of the I.M.S. — he had just come down from Wana on ten days' leave and Harry had asked him to look me up. He's very nice and terrific good fun. He used to be stationed in Pindi, and knows practically everyone here. He asked me out to dinner on Friday, and the fancy-dress dance on Saturday (yesterday). On Friday we went to Sam's (the only eating-place in Pindi apart from the club) and had a long and satisfactory talk about Harry, Wana, and so on.

4.

The fancy-dress dance was terrific fun. My Snow-White costume really looked very pretty, but no one seemed to have the slightest idea what I was meant to be. Most people asked if I was the Queen of Hearts or the Ace of Spades, or something equally ridiculous! John introduced me to a man called Bill Sutherland (a tall man who looked utterly stunning in cowboy outfit) who said he was going away for a week, but might he look me up when he came back!

Incidentally, I'm supposed to be half-Russian! I was in a party one night, I forget when, and happened to be talking about the 300 Club in Calcutta, and mentioned the Lissanewitches. Someone said "goodness, how can you twist your

136

5

tongue round a name like that?" and before
I could reply someone else piped up "Oh,
didn't you know, her father was Ambassador
to all the Russias, and married a Russian."
Of course, it was only a rather feeble
attempt to be funny but it was taken
quite seriously, so I played up and
spun a wonderful yarn about how lucky
my mother had been to marry an Englishman
and leave Russia before the revolution, and
how her poor brother Sergei (luckily I know
how to pronounce it) was butchered by
the Reds, another brother, Alexis, just
disappeared, we still don't know whether
he was killed or sent to Siberia, or just
starved, and my poor grandmother, the
Princess Tatiana Oniegine, barely escaped
with her life, smuggled out of the country by a

6.

faithful servant. Tell Mummy her name is really Valeny Alexandroovna! The result is, a lot of people call me "Russia" and one man told me, in all seriousness, that he would have guessed anyway that I was at least half-Russian because I had Russian eyes — no Englishwoman ever had eyes that were so lovely, so full of passion — !!!

I shall get most batts onely conceited in this place.

My fondest love to all, and don't keep this letter to yourself.

Cheery-bye.

Love,

Mary.

Metropole Hotel
Pindi.

6ᵗʰ April. 1939.

My darling Mummy,

I can't remember just where my last letter left off, but I think I told you about the fancy-dress ball on Saturday. Well, since that nothing very exciting has happened, because that finished Pindi Week, and this week half the population seems to be going down to Jhelum to take an exam. John Forster has gone for it, so has Terence Sharlock. However, to-night I am going to the cocktail dance with Capt. Ben Dryer, whom I have adored from afar ever since I arrived. Goodness knows why, he isn't handsome!

2.

The photographs of me at the races aren't particularly good, I'll send you the best one. Anyway, it looks cheerful, and is rather good of Major Geoffs, my escort — a very nice man. For pleasant companionship, give me the middle-aged bachelor every time.

I'm sure I have mentioned the Waltons — an extremely nice young couple that Harry introduced me to before he left. They asked me to spend the day with them yesterday — they live out at Chaklala. I went over for lunch and tea, and spent the afternoon playing engines with their three-year old son. After tea, we walked round their garden, and they picked masses of sweet-peas and carnations for me.

3.

They often send me flowers, which help to cheer up the rather dingy hotel rooms.

Harry rang up yesterday and said he had a good chance of getting ten days' leave at the end of this month. He has got a dachsund puppy for me — a brown one — by name, Becky Sharp, which he will bring down with him.

The weather here is absolutely ideal at the moment, not too hot during the day and pleasantly cool at night.

How's old Taylor behaving and have you found a way to leave the flat? Or have you got to stand by the three years on the lease?

This seems a very short and

4.

Scrappy letter, but I think I've told you all there is to be told! Perhaps there'll be more news next time.

I'm still waiting for the photos. so won't post this just yet.

With love to all,
            from
        Your loving daughter
                Mary

Metropole Hotel.
Pindi.
14th April 1939.

My dear Phyllis,

I've been wondering what sort of an Easter you've all been having! The newspaper says it has been a fine, warm one, that is something. And with Dick so near, am I right in taking it for granted there was a spot of whoopee?

I thought Easter here was going to be dreadful, as so many people seemed to be going away for it, however it cleared up so I went to the swimming pool at the club, where I had a gorgeous bathe and met Geoffs, who took me under his wing. He suggested we should take a picnic tea out to Wah gardens that afternoon. I'd never heard of them before, but agreed thankfully enough. The gardens turned out

2.

to be about 30 miles out on the Peshawar road. We passed the famous monument to John Nicholson on the way. The gardens were built — or planned — or whatever you do to gardens — hundreds of years ago as a resting-place for travellers and there are some ruins. They are quite large, shady and altogether lovely, though rather neglected. When we came back we discovered there was some quite amusing musical film on, so after dinner we went to that.

And that was my last outburst of gaiety in this place so famed for its "marvellous" times. However, Tomorrow (Saturday) I am going to the dance with Ben Dyer. I shall wear my butterfly net frock and make a whoopee night of it, as it will probably be the last big night at the club, for a great many of the women leave for Murree next week — indeed, some have already gone, I can't

3.

think why. After that one fine day of the picnic (Easter Sunday) it started raining again, and turned so cold that in a perfect fury I put my summer things back into the box and hauled out my warm frocks. However, yesterday it cleared up again, and to-day it is really quite hot, so I mean to go swimming again after tea. I am staying here till the 10th May, as Harry is hoping to get ten days' leave at the end of this month or the beginning of next month, so of course I don't want to go till he has been down here.

This is how I fill in my day. After breakfast, an hour with the munshi. Then I do the crossword puzzle, trying to make it last as long as possible. Then take Buttons for a walk, or go to the library to change my book, or do any little bits of shopping that may be necessary. These things have to fill the

4.

morning. After lunch (I spin meal-times out as long as possible) I write letters, read, and do half-an-hour or so of exercises. After tea another walk for Buttons, reading, mending, knitting and homework for the Munshi! Dinner 8.30. Listen to the news at 9.30. Smoke a bit - yawn a bit - decide there's nothing to do but go to bed!

The result is, when one _does_ go out to parties, one doesn't seem to have anything to talk about! However, now it's fine and warm, I shall spend a lot of time quite happily at the swimming-pool. And then, every now and then, one gets a spate of these morning tea-parties - there are _three_ next week.

My Munshi has just been - not for my lesson, I've already had that -

5.

but in order to tell me it is their New
Year Festival, and to bring me various
Indian sweets from the feast with which
they celebrate it. He kept saying "Taste
it! taste it!" so I couldn't very well
do otherwise, and of course I said everything
was quite delicious, but now that he's gone
it feels as if the skin's coming off my
tongue! Goth They were hot — peppery
heat, I mean of course. Some of the
sweet sweets were delicious; I enjoyed
those — but what he called the tasty
ones —! I've packed the bearer off
to get me gallons of tea — the Munshi's
parting shot was the information that
after eating Indian food, one should
<u>never</u> take a cold drink, because it
would make one's throat swell after all
those spices! Oh, dear, I'm simply

6.

dying for a lime squash with lots of ice in it !

Much love to Mummy and all of you.

Yours in torment !

Mary.

Metropole Hotel,

Murree

29ᵗʰ April 1939

Darling Mummy,

Thanks so much for your long letter and the snaps, they are good, especially the one of Angela balancing on the garden roller.

Notice the change of address! I came up here yesterday, as Bill Sutherland offered me a lift. He hasn't got a car himself, but was lent one by a friend, who asked us to come and have drinks on Thursday evening and collect the car at the same time. They had a "black-out" that night (yes, we have A.R.P. even out here) so we sat out in the garden watching the planes. There was bright moonlight, so the "raiders" must have had an easy time. Bill and I decided to

2.

go on to the Club for dinner. We met and
joined up with another party there – little
Tony Cowdray, who promised to come up to
Murree to see me, a man whose name I
never caught, and Major White – Tommy –
who sat opposite me at dinner, and poured
hock into my glass, murmuring the while
" Wonderful eyes – never seen anything like
them – pools – absolute pools." For the
rest of dinner he did nothing but murmur
" Pools – " to the vast delight of the
others, who wanted to know "pools
of what?" Various rude suggestions were
made, but it was eventually decided to
the satisfaction of all, that they must be
pools of vodka (my Russian ancestry
being firmly believed). The party then
became unduly hilarious, so Bill and I
slipped away, as we had previously

3.

decided to make it an early night, as we both had to pack the next day.

I spent the next morning frantically sorting and packing, and we set off after lunch. The car is only a small one, so the bearers and luggage had to follow on a bus. We had a picnic tea on the way. On arrival we found Murree damnably cold, and everyone wearing winter clothes. Bill dumped me at the hotel, then dashed off to look for the bungalow where he is staying. I phoned Harry and told him I'd arrived.

This morning while I was in the throes of unpacking, and cursing like fun because I had left nice warm Pindi, Bill suddenly appeared, and said the Chawners (the people he's staying with) asked me to dinner to-night, and what about coming along to meet Mrs. C.? So down we went (down

4

the right word, this hotel is the highest situated building in Murree — and how the wind whistles round it!) Mrs. C. is a very jolly woman, rather to doggy and horsey, but friendly enough. We had tea, then went into the garden and helped to paint her fence.

My quarters are rather pleasant, the sitting-room has the most glorious view. But none of the doors or windows fit properly, so it's very draughty. But it does make me cross to find it so cold, what's the use of coming out to India? I'm in two minds about packing up and going back to Pindi — only Pindi's so empty now.

That's all my news at the moment. Love to all, and thank Angela for her nice letter.

Your loving daughter,

Mary

Metropole Hotel,
Murree.
6th May 1939.

My dear Angela,

Very many happy returns of the day! You _are_ getting grown-up now, actually in your teens.

I'm afraid this letter will arrive a bit late, which isn't because I'd forgotten your birthday, but because I've been looking round for something to send you, but the shops up here are such potty little affairs I can't find anything at all nice. Never mind, wait till Christmas (yes, I know it's a long time ahead!)

I was pleased with your nice long letter. You seem to be a reformed

character these days, I've just had a
letter from Phyllis in which she tells
me you are being positively angelic!
Shabash! Which means "well done."

There isn't anything to tell you
because Murree is a deadly hole, and
I have nothing to do but take the
dog for walks, and get books from
the library. Murree is built on several
hills, one is either walking uphill or
downhill all the time, and believe me,
they are jolly steep hills, too! But
the views are marvellous, miles and
miles of pine-clad hills, and snow-
clad mountains in the distance. It's
lovely and warm during the day, but
very cold at night. They have electric

3.

light here, but it has a charming habit of failing — all of a sudden the lights twinkling on the hills disappear, and your own room is plunged in darkness, so that you have to grope for matches and candles and wait — sometimes for half-an-hour — for the light to come on again.

Everyone was very excited yesterday because there was an earthquake. Tremor during the night, but I was asleep and it didn't wake me. No damage was done, apart from a few things falling off tables, etc.

I have bought myself a sketch-book and some water-colours, and amuse myself by trying to sketch the really lovely scenery, but I'm afraid my

4.

attempts are pathetic, I'm sure you could do better !!

Murree is very dull, however it's not for long, because Harry's leave is due on the 15th June and then we are going to Kashmir — we have booked a house-boat on the Dal Lake, that will be great fun.

Harry often mentions you in his letters, and tells me to be sure and send you his love. He would like to write to you and Mummy and Phyllis, but is so busy (besides his own work he has to do that of a man who has gone on leave) that he only writes me very short letters.

With much love from
Your loving sister,
Mary

Metropole Hotel.
Murree.
23rd May 1939.

Darling Flip,

I do feel most awfully guilty, I know I haven't written for ages! Do forgive me — I seem to lurch from one beat-up to another, and don't have time for anything.

How are you after your operation? Has it made you feel really well again? Incidentally, it's ages since I've heard from any of you, do tell me all about things. Did Dick come to see you in hospital?

Harry rang up yesterday and said his leave had been cancelled, just imagine how utterly sickening! However, I was rung up by the hotel this morning when I was at some beer-party in Lintott's, and

157

2.

told that a call had come through for me
from Dara. I almost ran back to the
Metropole (¼ hour's walk, all uphill!)
and when Harry got through again, he
said he thought he might be getting it
after all, only from the end of June
instead of the middle.

There's a whole crowd of people here
on an Intelligence Course, and most of
them manage to get away in time to
drink beer at Lintott's by 12.30 every
morning. One or two of them are staying
at the Metropole — they had to draw a
map for their homework the other day, and
I drew Pip Burrough's for him, because
he had had such a thick night the night
before, he just couldn't cope! He was
so pleased he promised me a bottle of
champagne next time we met in the club,

3.

but I've often seen him there since, and the champagne hasn't materialised yet! Anyway, I've had quite enough without any from Pip.

There is a lad up here in the Worcesters, called Theo Clarke, whom I met in Pindi on the night of the fancy-dress. He always calls me "Snow-White" and the result is, everyone here now calls me that! (Incidentally the Russian story is still going strong).

25ᴿ

Yesterday was one long alcoholic maze, haze, or whatever you like to call it. I was having a quiet drink with one or two of the Intelligentsia, as I call them, when along came Tommy White (the one who said my eyes were "pools, pools — ") and a man called John Bramfield,

4.

and asked me to have lunch with them at Sam's. That meant more drink while waiting for our lunch, hock with it, and liqueurs afterwards. We eventually finished about 4 pm. and I took a rickshaw home (I needed it!) I slept till 6.30, and at 7.30 was out on another party with a man called Curly (Donald Brenner). We dined at the club where there was a dance in progress, and joined up with Theo Clarke and a girl called Riki. Curly is priceless. He sat down under a potted palm, the fronds of which came right down into his eyes, so he called a bearer, who, with perfect solemnity, trimmed the palm with a large pair of scissors, while Curly sat back looking like an Eastern Potentate and everyone in the room had hysterics.

5.

Tonight I am dining and dancing at Brightlands with Tommy White, John B., Nena Morgan and Beryl Harris (two extremely nice sisters, both married and fellow – grass widows) and a nice youngster called Peter Ommanny. It will be a champagne party – most parties up here are.

Last Sunday I went out with Theo Clarke. We went on Tats, with coolies to carry our lunch. We rode miles, and found a lovely place for lunch. But almost anywhere's a lovely place for a picnic up here, with all these beautiful pine forests. We couldn't find a suitable place for a canter (to my secret relief) but the Trot soon came back to me, though I was just bounced anyhow at first. Harry tells me

6.

this Arab grey he has got for me
(Sir Galahad) is rather frisky and Takes
a bit of managing, so I'll have to
learn properly before I can compete with
that !

The last person to write to me was
Angela, who sent me such a nice letter.
When are the rest of you cads going
to write ?

My love to Mummy, Teddy,
Angela and yourself.

Your loving sister,

Mary.

Nagin Bagh.
25th June 1939.

My dear Phyllis,

Well, here we are on a houseboat in Kashmir! We came up here about a week ago, and have been dashing round looking for a good place to moor our houseboat. This lake — the Nagin Bagh — is utterly lovely. It is fringed with willows and poplars, and behind our moorings are orchards of plums and cherries and apricots. Opposite is a range of mountains, and on a clear day one can see another range beyond, which is snow-covered all the year round.

2.

We spent a week in Murree before coming up here. I meant to dash round introducing Harry to all my friends but I never got a chance as there was a 'flu epidemic and I got it! Harry luckily escaped. I made a very quick recovery, however.

The road up here is simply hair-raising, all except the last forty miles (out of 160 miles) is winding along the sides of steep hills with a terrific drop on one side — most of the time with a turbulent river (the Jhelum) at the

3.

foot of the hill. The road is also very narrow and the surface bad. But the scenery magnificent.

You can all expect a surprise in about a month or six weeks' time! Birthday and Christmas presents combined — and perhaps next birthdays as well — as you will understand when you see what you get !! The only problem is Teddy, as we cannot find a suitable present for a man. Please explain to him what a lot of puzzlement he is causing us, and ask him for suggestions ! The things are

4.

all being specially made — They
are only made to order — that's
why you must wait so long.
However we are pretty sure you will
think these things worth waiting for!
No, I shall not tell you — !

The club is on the opposite side
of the lake. There is tennis and
ping-pong there and dances twice a
week, but we are leading a
quiet life. There is also bathing
at the club and of a boat in
the middle of the lake. That
must sound odd, but the lake
is so full of weeds that it

5.

is dangerous to bathe except in those two place where the weeds are specially cleared away. We also have a small boat which we paddle ourselves. It's all great fun and the houseboat is comfortable if cramped, and I'm getting quite good at ordering meals! although somewhat handicapped by the fact that it is impossible to get beef here, as the Maharajah is a very strict Hindu and won't allow even tinned beef to be sold. However, with duck, chicken, mutton and fish one rings the changes adequately

6.

and the fruit here is varied and extremely good — the mangoes are enormous and the best I've ever tasted!

Harry was looking very pale and thin when he arrived, but is looking much better now. Your letter amused him, particularly as you appeared to forget the last page - it wasn't finished, anyway!

I hope Mummy and everyone are well. Love to all and show them this letter.

With love from
Mary.

c/o Lloyds Bank Ltd.
The Bund,
Srinagar
Kashmir.
8th July 1939.

My dear Mummy,

We are still on the Nagin Bagh, and having a pretty good time, as people we know keeping come up here and we know quite a crowd now. However, we have only had one hectic party, the day before yesterday. They got up a Swimming Gala at the club annexe out here, and it was the grandest fun.

First of all several boats collected at an ~~other~~ far corner of the Lake, one boat containing

2.

Neptune with attendant lovelies.
His boat was hung with weed
from the Lake. Another boat contained
Britannia, also with lovelies (I was
one, in a long white muslin frock
with garlands of red and blue).
There were also several boatloads
of pirates. Harry was a pirate,
with skull and cross bones on his
chest drawn with burnt cork,
and hearts Transfixed with arrows,
drawn with lipstick on his arms.
The boats at a given signal
moved off to the club bathing
pier, where, Britannia and Neptune
were received by an Admiral,
Mrs. Grundy and some vague
person who garlanded them and

3.

led them to their thrones. Then two of the pirates were caught flirting with the lovelies by Mrs. Grundy, who expressed her horror at such disgraceful behaviour, and caused them to be thrown in the lake. Harry was one of them. Then, I, alas! was found flirting with Neptune — who was much enjoying it — and was also thrown into the lake, and had to be helped out again as my long skirt wrapped itself round my feet and I couldn't swim! There were then various swimming races, which neither of us went in for, as I was desperately trying to get my hair dry in time for the parade

4.

of bathing belles, and Harry was busy removing his burnt cork and lipstick, as he also was to appear as a bathing-belle!! He wore a green bathing costume lent to by some girl, with socks in the right place to represent a bosom — lots of make-up and a hanky tied round his head to hide deficiencies of hair! I wore a flat straw hat tied on by ribbon, which did help a bit to hide the state of my hair — anyway, I won first prize! After the parade Mrs. Grundy was stripped and thrown into the water by the bathing-belles — who objected to her comments on the modern girl —

5.

and then an imposter was discovered! — who was also thrown in. When he emerged from the water he was seen to remove and wring out his bust — which delighted the spectators. When all the swimming and diving was over, people adjourned to the club house, and prizes were distributed. Mine was a lovely little scent spray with a green tassel, and a bottle of Potter and Moore's lavender scent. People then returned to their houseboats to change and dine, and after dinner there was a dance at the club which was pretty hectic and went on till all hours. You see,

6.

all the dances at the club
annexe are to a gramophone
with loudspeakers round the room,
as the place isn't considered large
enough to warrant the expense of
a band. Well, with a gramophone
you can go on as long as you
want to!

The next day (yesterday) we
went over to the club in the
morning to recuperate with the gentle
aid of brandies - and - ginger-ale.
There we heard rather startling news.
No less than five people - all
friends of ours - had been recalled
and were to leave at once, one
of them to go overseas "to an
unknown destination." These five in

7.

addition to John Motley, who was supposed to come and join us for a month — we have a spare room — and wired at the last moment to say he couldn't come — he had been recalled to his regiment. There's obviously something odd in the wind, but Harry has asked me to ask you not to talk about this.

Several photographs were taken of the Swimming Gala, and we shall be sending you a batch of prints in a few days' time. We are going to take a snap of this houseboat too, so that you can see what the things

8.

look like ! Ours has the extraordinary name of "Betel Guest " !

We were sorry to hear Phyllis had been having ulcers in her throat — she told me this in her last letter. Does it mean that the broken needle is working its' way through ? I must say I am very anxious to hear what happens about this. It must be terribly worrying for you.

Much love to all. Your presents are nearly ready !

With lots of love,
from
Mary.

H.B. Betel Guest,

26⁵ Aug. 1939.

My dear Mummy,

I'm afraid it's a shockingly long time since I last wrote! We went out on a nine-days trek from the Wular Lake, up the road to Gilgit. We had to cross a pass at 11,000 ft.! And was it cold! The scenery was magnificent and one could see incredible distances — right down to the Wular Lake, sixteen miles away, and across and beyond it — and the Lake is ten miles broad at least! As we crossed the pass the Lake was hidden from view, but we then came in sight of the most gorgeous ranges of snow-capped mountains — and didn't we just get an icy wind blowing off them! The road was a mere track, which most of the time crawled along the sides of mountains, with a sheer drop on one side! The first day we

2.

did sixteen miles and reached Tragbal, 9,200 ft. high. We spent a day there, it was so lovely up there among the pines. Then we pushed on to Karakbal, 15 miles, crossing the pass and coming to a region where the hills were streaked with glaciers, and there were streams in every valley. The next day we reached Badwan where we camped for two days.

Badwan was a pretty little valley full of trout streams, but, alas! the license was far too expensive for us to fish.

When we got back, we went to Ali Joo, the furriers, to ask about your coat, and to our fury and indignation we found it hadn't yet been dyed, in fact they hadn't even started on it. We gave them a hell of a ticking-off, but I'm afraid it means you won't get

3.

your coat till some time in October, as fur takes a long time to dye. I do hope you can manage with an old coat till then.

<u>29ᵗʰ Aug</u>

Very pleased to get Phyllis' letter and hear that her fur has arrived, but we are worried about Angela's present, which was posted before Phyllis'! And hasn't Teddy's arrived yet either? Angela's present is a wool dressing-gown — pashmina wool — very soft and light — beautifully embroidered. Teddy's present is a table-lamp and book-ends in walnut to match with his initials carved on them. If we don't hear soon that they have arrived we will claim on the post-office, as everything was registered.

I'm afraid it's a shockingly long time since I last wrote. We have been caught up in a series

4.

of parties which begin with golf before lunch and end with vingt-et-un at midnight !! When we first got back from trek we got involved with a party of Americans who were terrific beaters-up — they <u>were</u> a nice crowd — and as soon as they had gone we ran into Casey Khanna, an Indian officer whom I had met in Murree. He and another Indian called Dewan (whom I nicknamed Groucho because he looks just like Groucho Marx) and two girls called Doreen Lewis and Peggy Peerless have been making a six-some for a series of terrific parties. Incidentally Casey is going to England for his two month's leave next year so I have given him Phyllis' address at Imperial Airways, as I didn't know whether you'd still be in the same flat — I thought probably not if you could possibly get out of it !

5.

He's a very nice lad and perfectly English in manners, speech, and outlook. I'm sure you'll like him.

Harry has just heard that after his three months' M.T. course in Pindi he is going to Peshawur, and has received his application form for a married officer's bungalow. However, it's no use getting thrilled about it, as there is no knowing what will happen if war breaks out, and really one cannot see how it can be averted. It's horrible to think we may already be at war by the time you get this letter. I wish to God you were farther out of London.

Tomorrow we are going down to Pindi, where our address will be :—

Glenview Hotel, Magdala Road.

With lots of love

from your loving daughter

Mary.

Glenview Hotel,
Magdala Rd.
Pind.
7th Sept. 1939.

Dear Teddy,
Thanks for your letter, I'm so glad the presents arrived safely, we appear to have sent them off just in time!

You were lucky to get of Germany by the last train! Being interned wouldn't be a bit funny. Thanks for the snaps, they are lovely, we hope to be sending you our snaps of Kashmir soon. The one you sent of a stream tumbling over rocks between fir trees is very like parts of Kashmir, except that the bridge in the background is too solid; most of the bridges we crossed consisted of loose planks laid across the supporting beams. Planks were often missing, and then it was an awful business getting the pack ponies to cross the gap. As for your 9,000 ft. – pooh! – we crossed a pass at 11,000 ft.!

2.

It's pretty hot down here, 100° or 101° by day and 85° by night; that may not sound much, but none of the hotels or bungalows here have ceiling fans, and the little table fans aren't nearly so effective. One needs at least four cold baths a day!

The other evening we went out for a drive just to get some fresh air and our car suddenly caught fire. We smothered the engine with earth, and dolefully pushed the car back into the hotel compound. The next morning she was collected by the garage-men, and the garage kindly lent us another car. Unfortunately that very same day we gave a friend a lift to the station, and just as we reached the station that car too went up in flames! Neither car was seriously damaged, however.

The temperature has now gone up to 103° ! Phew !!

3.

As there is nothing for me to do when Harry is at the school, I am having lessons in Urdu. I can speak a fair amount now, but will need to know it a great deal better to run a bungalow — if we ever get one! Also, although it is not necessary, I am learning the writing, which is fascinating but difficult. There seem to be about six different ways of writing each letter, and letters we haven't got in our alphabet ﻋﺴ, for instance, which equals "sh". It is also written from right to left.

Please thank Angela for her most amusing letter, and give my love to Mummy and Phyllis.

Your affectionate sister,
Mary.

P.S.   I enclose a pleasing little verse I heard the other day. It'll pass right over Phyllis' head, but I'm sure you'll appreciate it!

Glenview Hotel,
Magdala Road,
Rawalpindi.
11th Sept. 1939.

My dear Mummy,
     Goodness knows how long this letter
will take to reach you, as the air mail
is now a prohibitive price, and I'm told
the sea-mail has to go all the way
round the Cape!
     However, there is very little to
tell you. Harry has started on the
M.S. course, and we are quite pleased
with this hotel. Pindi is very dull
and empty, but thank heaven, it is
now much cooler. The days seem endless,
as there is absolutely nothing for me to
do when Harry is at work. When he
comes back, he gives me a driving
lesson, then we listen to the news on
the wireless. Sometimes we go to the
Club for a drink and to discuss
the news with other people.
     I wish to goodness I knew how
you are getting on at home. Phyllis

185

2.

told me in her last letter she would
have to leave Imperial Airways if there
was a war, so I suppose by now
she is in some Women's Auxiliary Force
by now. And I don't suppose she'll
earn enough in that to be able to
help you any more. I quite realise
it's a patriotic, not a money-making,
career, but that doesn't alter the
fact that it's hard on you. Teddy
must have been called up, too, though
goodness knows what as, since he's
as blind as a bat even with glasses.
So Harry and I picture you and
Angela alone in the flat, and wonder
if Angela is still able to go to
school, or if it has closed down
being so near London?

    I wish to God I was at home
now and able to do something,
instead of leading the futile, empty
life of an Army wife out here.
Here one can only devise methods
of killing time — stupid methods

3.

like Mah-johngg or golf — and if only I'd stayed at home, I might have done something helpful — A. R. P. work, or something.

I think the Army contains the dullest men and the stupidest women in the world. The men have two topics of conversation — horses - and shop. The women have one — did Mrs. Blank go to bed with Lt. Snooks or not? One can hardly blame the women for their dullness, though, considering the boredom of their lives.

Sorry to unload such a grumble on to you! but it drives me really crazy twiddling my thumbs out here instead of doing something at home. And Pindi is so boring. In Calcutta one met business people — of all nationalities, — artists, I.C.S., police, here there is nothing but army — army — army.

To-night we are going to be devils and go to the flicks.

Much love,

Mary.

Glenview Hotel,
Magdala Road,
Rawalpindi.

21st September, 1939.

My dear Mummy,

Thank you so much for your airmail letter, I'll
send this airmail too, as my last letter may have just
missed the last of the airmails.

Harry has been recalled to Wana.   Isn't it utterly
sickening?   All the R.I.A.S.C. people on the M.T. course
were recalled, there are only a few cavalry people left
taking a short course.   The infuriating thing is,
Harry 'phoned me up when he reached Wana, and said
nobody up there had the faintest idea why these people
should be recalled, as what frontier trouble there had
been was now all over, and anyway it wasn't anywhere
near Wana!   They say the A.D.S.& T. concerned is a windy
old woman.   So many of them are.

I've been killing time one way and another.   Urdu
lessons, driving lessons, a flick or two.   I usually
go down to the club for a swim after tea.   Tim Grey, of
the Worcestershires, and John Phillips of the Guides,
have been giving me driving lessons, and I have started
driving by myself - though I haven't got a licence yet!

22nd Sept.

I was interrupted yesterday by a man called Bill
Sealey, a very old friend of Harry's.   He was very
disappointed not to see Harry; he has just come down
from the Frontier, and must have just missed him.
Anyway, I rang Harry up last night from the club, as
this wretched hotel isn't on the 'phone yet, and there
was Bill again having a drink on the club lawn, so he
asked me to join him while I was waiting for my call
to come through, and go on to Sam's and the flicks with
him afterwards.   We went to Sam's and played fruit
machines, and he insisted on having a large bottle of
champagne with dinner as it was his first beat-up since
coming down from Mir Ali.   Well, I don't mind helping
people celebrate, when the celebration takes the form
of champagne!   However, a large bottle between only
two people takes some drinking and by the time we'd
finished it, it was too late for the flicks so we went

- 2 -

to the club instead, where we met John Phillips and
joined up with him.   There isn't much to do here at
the moment except go to the flicks, because dancing
doesn't start till the end of next month.   However,
I suppose you think we're pretty lucky even to have
the flicks to go to! as the papers say that every
kind of entertainment has been closed down in and
round London.   Does that even apply as far aut as
Beckenham?

Have prices gone up in England?   They're soaring
here, in spite of attempts to keep down profiteering.
It isn't that' there's any difficulty in getting things
yet, but the beastly shopkeepers think war is an
excellent excuse for putting up prices.

Please tell Phyllis that I have just got her airmail letter, and will be answering it in a day or two.
In future my letters also will be sea-mail.   But what
on earth is Phyllis going to do, now that she's lost
her job because of the wretched war, and can't get any
war work?   It seems very odd to me that the woman
recruiting officer Phyllis interviewed should have
told her they didn't want any more girls, and then a
few days later there was an announcement that they were
taking on hundreds more as they stillhadn't got enough!
She seems to have been a very rude and discouraging sort
of woman - most unsuitable for a recruiting officer!
Has Phyllis tried to get any A.R.P. work, or is that
all voluntary?   What's worrying me is that if Phyllis
can't get any paid work, your finances are going to be
in a pretty awful state, aren't they?   Particularly
if Teddy is called up too, as I suppose he must be.
I wish to goodness we could help, but I'm afraid it
just isn't possible, we're rather in the soup ourselves
after three months in Kashmir!

We've got rather a good reason now to want to put by
some money, if we can manage it.   I wonder if you'll be
pleased to hear that you are an expectant grandmother!!!
I simply can't imagine you as a granny - you look so
ridiculously young that no-one will believe it.   But I
can't imagine myself as a fond mamma either.   However,
there it is, and it should be arriving in March - end of
March.   And neither of us cares a hoot whether it's a
girl or a boy.   A boy will be called "Anthony" - we both
like the name "Tony" - and a girl will be called either
"Rosemary" or "Margaret", we're not quite sure which.

- 3 -

If it's "Rosemary", Angela of course must be one of the godmothers - how would she like that? I feel very fit and full of beans, so there's no need to worry about me.

Well, that *is* news for you, isn't it? I hope you will all be as pleased about it as we are.

Much love to all. Oh, and please tell Angela she can send that dressing-gown to the laundry as often as she pleases, pashmina wool washes beautifully, and the embroidery is in fast colours. I'm afraid your present will be a long time arriving if it has to go round the Cape. It isn't quite finished yet, but we didn't dare make too much of a fuss about it, in case it should not be cured properly if we tried to hurry them. Better to wait a bit longer and be sure of well-cured skins! Cheer up, you'll get it sometime!

Your loving daughter,

Mary

P.S. I keep forgetting to tell you — I never received a penny from the people you mentioned when I got married. Could you find out about it from your end? No one here seems to know anything about it. Incidentally, if you're not too broke! — could you send me some "Luckstone" for a Christmas present? I've nearly finished mine & it does make such a difference to one's complexion out here. White, please, with the carnation scent.

190

Shore's Hotel,
Napier Road,
Rawalpindi.

24th Oct. 1939.

My dear Mummy,

Thank you so much for your airmail letter, I'll
send this one airmail too, as I haven't written for
some time.   After that I'll write sea-mail, but more
regularly!

I really haven't known during the past six weeks
whether I've been coming or going, or rather, whether
Harry has, as he's been dashing backwards and forwards
between Wana and Pindi in the most bewildering way.
Coming down here ~~~~~~~~~~~~~~~~~~~ - I don't know what - going
back to Wana - sent down here - recalled to Wana - and
now here he is again, this time for seven weeks on a
course - unless he's recalled again!

You will also see that I've moved to another
hotel, the food in the Glenview was too appalling.
It's very good here, and the quarters are comfortable,
though smaller.   Still, with the cold weather coming
on, that's an advantage.   It's beginning to turn quite
chilly here at night, and I had every excuse for wearing
my fur coat at the dance last Saturday.   We are
continually writing to Ali Joo in Srinagar to tell them
to buck up with your coat, and Harry has now cancelled
a cheque he gave them for something else, and told them
they will get nothing till your coat is ready and has
been approved of.   We are hoping it will arrive in
time for Christmas.   I suppose we had better send it
to Auntie Dot's, as it seems likely you will be going
there; if you're not there, at any rate she will always
know where to send it.

Harry arrived about tea-time last Saturday, having
rung me up from D. I. K. the previous night to warn me
of this sudden posting.   I was already booked to go out
to dinner and dance, in a party with the Chrismans (who
are in Attock oil).   I had a mah-johngg party on
Saturday morning to which Stella Chrisman was coming,
so I was able to explain the situation to her, and of

I'm told the censor wouldn't pass that bit.

191

- 2 -

course she extended the invitation to Harry. We had a
very merry little dinner at their bungalow first, and
gathered round the piano and sang rude songs, led by
Peggy Morrell, who used to be a crooner in somebody's
band. We got to the club about 11, and the dance
finished at twelve, so I only had four dances, but
actually was rather relieved that the dance should
finish so early, as I get tired very easily, which I
suppose is only to be expected. (Anyway, I don't show
a thing yet, though it's four months). Isn't it absurd,
though, the club is not allowed to put on dances later
than 12.30, and there are to be no regimental dances or
cocktail parties, and large private cocktail parties or
parties at the club, will be "regarded with disfavour".
Fancy-dress dances are also "unsuitable". This is
because of the way. It would give the impression we
were not "taking the war seriously". Well, what better
impression could we possibly give!! And all the
unfortunate lads who may be shot off home or to Egypt
at any moment, are only allowed to enjoy themselves in
a quiet, demure and decorous manner. Most senior
officers have been dead and stuffed for a long time,
it's about time someone realised it and put them in a
museum.

I've been driving the car quite a lot, and by
myself too, I'm hoping to take the test some time next
week.

A sea-mail letter from Phyllis arrived the other
day, but she says in it she is still looking for a job,
so I don't know what the job is that you mention in
your airmail letter. I'm sorry it's such a poor one.
Give Phyllis my love, and say I'll write to her next.
Surely she'll get a better one later on, they'll be
needing more and more girls as the war goes on.

It seems very remote out here, this war, and to
tell the truth, very dull. The news on the wireless
and in the paper always seems to be the same. But
no-one seems to expect it to last long, that's one
consolation. Why hasn't Teddy been called up, or has
he by now?

Thanks awfully for offering to send me your old
cot-sheets and baby-clothes. I'd love anything in
the way of clothes (it doesn't matter if they're long,
they can be cut down), but for cot-sheets I mean to use

- 3 -

pashmina, which is wool but as smooth as linen, and
quite cheap out here. You can imagine the pile of
knitting I have on hand; I bought a stock of wool
quickly, before the prices had time to go up.   I am
now working on a pink cot blanket or pram-cover.   It
is knitted in very thick wool, and will be bound with
wide ribbon or taffeta, with an appliqued rabbit or
something of the sort in one corner.   Pink is supposed
to be for a girl, so out of sheer perversity the thing
will probably turn out to be a boy.   Not that I care
which it is!   Have you told Angela yet that she is to
be godmother?   Norah Foss has agreed to stand proxy.

Harry sends his love to all.   I won't be so long
writing again!

Much love from

Your loving daughter,

Mary

Shore's Hotel
Napier Road
Rawalpindi

26th November 1939

My dear Flip,

I wonder what you're doing today to celebrate your birthday!

I had been saying some hard things about you, but I take them back now as I have just had two letters from you by the same post. They were dated a fortnight apart, which shows how eccentric the mail is these days!

Your job certainly doesn't sound inspiring, let's hope Longhurst's efforts are successful. It is kind of him.

The day before yesterday the RIASC mess gave a cocktail dance and we went with a Capt. Butter, who's on the same course as Harry, and a girl called Peggy Peerless who lives in this hotel. It was the first dance we'd been to for over a month, and we did enjoy it. I wore my net frock and jade earrings (Harry' Christmas present in advance!). It was nice to find I can still wear an evening dress without embarrassment, I really don't show a thing although it's now five months! I give the impression I've got a bit fatter, that's all. It was much nicer than the club dances, much cosier and friendlier, and everyone knew everyone, and there were lovely big fires to gather round when not dancing, and masses of those delicious cocktail savouries, a weakness of mine!

As for Christmas presents, Mummy suggested a dressing jacket in her last letter, I'd simply love one. I was going to knit myself one, but really I have as much

knitting as I can cope with, things for the infant and
Harry has demanded some more socks! It doesn't matter
what colour you send as my nighties are all colours. As
for Harry, he refused to suggest anything luckily I know
what he wants. Please send him some good linen hankies,
the dhobi has ruined his and we can only get such coarse,
rough ones here. Hankies sound a dull present but it's
a different matter when they're difficult to get! I can
assure you they would be welcomed with joy!

I   t's turned frightfully cold and so dry and dusty at
the same time that we have to put olive oil in our baths to
prevent our skins cracking! It's just nice during the day,
not too cold, and bright and sunny, but the temperature
drops 40 degrees at night!!

W   e had an earth quake the other day that lasted
six minutes. Harry timed it. It was a very gentle one
didn't do any damage, but it was a most peculiar sensation
to feel the floor shaking under one's feet and to see the
electric light bulb suddenly swing round and round and
hear the glass rattling like mad, and all for no apparent
reason!

I   still spend most of my mornings playing mah-
jong, which I mean to teach you all when I'm next at home.
It's fascinating and it's a pity to waste that nice set
Auntie Lucy gave us ages ago! I'm also playing golf pretty
regularly, but only a few holes of course I can't do the
whole course.

        Poor Harry is suffering from the most frightful
rash, which he caught from his mules. He is covered in it
from head to foot and it itches like mad. Fortunately it
is neither infectious nor contagious, so I am quite safe!
You can only get it from mules or horses and then only if

your skin is particularly sensitive, it's peculiar to a few people, and of course Harry would be one of them! At the present moment he's peeling, which thank goodness is the final stage. Otherwise he's well and sends his love to you all.

Much love to all, your loving sister.
Mary.

Shore's Hotel,
Napier Rd,
Pindi.
7ᵗʰ Dec. '39.

My dear Mummy,
I've just been spending a week in
hospital! Don't be alarmed, I haven't lost
the infant, it was only for an antrim puncture
— which proved to be unnecessary! About a
week ago I had a little mark, which looked
as if it were going to be a boil on my
nose; the next day the mark had spread,
the whole right side of my face was red
and swollen and painful, so we went to the
doctor who said it was fish-poisoning and
packed me off to bed with medicine and
a diet. Next morning both sides of my
face were swollen, so that it looked like
a big red football! The doctor promptly
sent me to the hospital, saying he now
considered it a case for the Ear, Nose &
Throat Specialist. Ever been inside a
military hospital? <u>Wonderful</u> places!

2.

The procedure is as follows: You own doctor tells you to see Major Somebody. You do. He asks you your name, your husband's rank, etc, then says "Does it hurt?" I said with much feeling that it did. Whereupon he prodded it, and remarked that I'd better see So-and-so. When we had seen all the So-and-sos in the hospital, who all did exactly the same, a sister took us in charge, said she'd been told I was to be admitted, and my room was ready. The next morning I was told to get up and dress as I must be over at the E.N.J. specialist's place at 9.30 am sharp. I was — but he wasn't. At 11.30 I eventually had the antrum puncture done. Most unpleasant. They push cocaine up your nose first to deaden the pain, then they put a long sharp instrument up one nostril and bore a hole through the bone at the top. You can hear the bone go "crunch" as it goes way. Then they wash out the inside of

3.

all those hollow bones. I'm afraid I passed right out, but apparently it's quite usual with an antrum puncture. My grumble is, that instead of getting on with the job while I was nicely unconscious (without costing the Government anything for anaesthetics!) they carefully brought me round, and then proceeded with their horrid work! And after all that, it wasn't necessary, they found my antrum was beautifully clean and quite, quite innocent — I was then told to go back to bed (I was supposed to be a stretcher case. I don't know why; anyway, they hadn't warned me, so I walked back and put myself to bed). Then they started a course of tablets which necessitated a strict diet; nothing seemed to be allowed except toast and/or chicken. (no vegetables with it!) And announced that they had engaged a private nurse for me as I required more treatment than the nursing sisters could cope with (lazy devils — all I had was nasal douches

4

and inhalations three times a day — and I had
to pay a private nurse for *That* !) Anyway,
the inflammation steadily went down, and they
let me go this morning, after x-raying my
teeth, just to make sure. Well, I'm home
now. anyway, and very glad about it, too,
though extremely worried about the expense
of that wretched nurse.

Your last letter seemed much more
cheerful than the previous ones! We were
so glad to notice it. After all, I don't
think you're likely to need that Air Raid
Shelter in the garden — do you remember
that evening when I was at home when
all the inhabitants of No 44 got
together and discussed digging a trench
or something? And of course it never
got done.

Mrs. Carre's remark about your
"well-off" son-in-law is distinctly
funny, but it won't do you any

5.

harm to let people think so, people being
the curious creatures that they are. I <u>do</u>
hope your coat won't take ages to get
home, I'm dying to imagine that you're
wearing it! Does Phyllis wear her furs
much? And she does understand, doesn't
she, that they were combined birthday-
and Christmas? All the presents were,
as we rather let ourselves go over them.

We have some cheerful news too.
Harry applied for ten days' leave at
Christmas — he will be here till the
21st anyway — and his application has
been "recommended" or something — anyway
it means he's likely to get it. I'm
knitting him socks for his Christmas
present — by request! So you can
imagine the welter of knitting I have
on hand at the moment!

6.

I attended one Red Cross meeting before going into hospital, but it was such an obvious waste of time, I doubt if I'll go again. We spent the entire morning sewing beads round bits of muslin "to cover milk-jugs." Well, the Pudi Branch works only for Indian troops, who are not given milk-jugs. Officers have trays with milk-jugs, but even they are not given milk-jug covers, and the troops are just given their mug of tea. So it was a completely wasted morning, and anyway could hardly be dignified by the name of "war-work." But the Commissioner's wife and the General's wife must have something to organise, poor dears!

    Much love to all from both of us.

        Your loving daughter,

          Mary.

P.S.   I still look like a country lass, with plump, red cheeks! But they're not painful any longer.

Shore's Hotel,
Napier Rd.
Pindi.
19th Dec. '39.

My dear Flip,

Thanks so much for your long letter, I would like to send this airmail, as I realise I have left Christmas greetings till too late, but we are too broke for airmail at the moment! So my best wishes to you all for 1940 instead!

We have been in a state of dither for the last few days wondering whether Harry was going to get his ten days' leave for Christmas — if he didn't get it, it meant leaving three days before Christmas. 31st Dec.

Positive whirl — <u>not</u> of gaiety — since starting this letter. First of all, a Red Cross Bazaar. The bazaar itself was quite good fun, but I was working all

2.

the morning making out receipts, checking over money for tickets, etc. I've come to the conclusion I'm the only woman with a business head in Pindi, since I'm always being asked to do things like that, or odd spots of Typing, for females who go into a flat spin and make five minutes' work last half an-hour and exhaust them !!

The next evening we took some flowers down to a woman from the hotel who had had a baby about a week previously, and arrived an hour after she died ! God, it was a shock. We had to take charge of the distraught husband, who didn't know what he was saying or doing, and drove him round to various friends he wanted to tell about it, and to the padre's, and arrange for a dose of morphia from the B. M. H. to put him to sleep for the night. The next day Harry had to make all the funeral arrangements the next day — because we

3.

helped the unfortunate husband out the first day, people seemed to expect us to take charge altogether, though we weren't really particular friends. It was even suggested that I should take charge of the baby – this little idea was very firmly and promptly squashed, since it was obviously a job for a woman who already had an infant and an ayah. Then for the next few days the husband, or rather widower, kept coming round, and though one sympathised with his desire for companionship, he was most difficult to talk to. Thank goodness he has now gone to stay with friends.

Anyway Harry got his leave and Christmas itself was good fun. Do you remember Harry and I staying for the night with some friends of Harry's down in Aldershot? They were John and Betty Barham. John has been here (in this hotel) for some time, and Betty arrived last week, plus infant, and full of good advice for me. I like Betty awfully, as am very thrilled about her

4.

arrival. The four of us went to the Christmas Eve dance. I didn't dance much, of course, but it was nice to go to the club again and watch the other couples dancing. John had a bottle of champagne, too, to celebrate Betty's arrival. I looked quite presentable in a frock with a full skirt.

5th Jan.

What a life! Christmas Day was quite good fun, we spent the morning with the Hayes and went to the flicks in the afternoon. The next day Harry didn't feel so good, and the following day retired to bed with fever. He stayed in bed till New Years' Eve getting steadily worse and was then removed to hospital in an ambulance. So you can now understand the interruption to this letter! Honestly, I seemed to spend my time changing bed sheets or supporting him to the bathroom! They have tested him

5.

for malaria, typhoid and enteric and can find no bugs. At one time they thought it was pleurisy because he was finding it difficult and painful to breathe and had a pain in his side. However, this evening his temperature is down, he is much better, and they think after all it was only a bad go of 'flu (which I said all along!). They're bound to give him a few days' convalescent leave.

As well as this, I've had to take Betty under my wing as she can't speak a word of Urdu yet & is always appealing for help with the bearer or ayah or someone. In return she bullies me into taking a walk every day. The manufacture of small garments makes slow but sure progress; as am I busy!

Please don't buy the cot as we can have one made out here by a

6.

Chinese carpenter, which will take to pieces – very necessary when you consider the amount of travelling one does, or is liable to do, out here. Up to the hills and back, for one thing. But prams are a difficulty. Could you send us the money, then we could use it for a very nice second-hand pram we have been offered at a reasonable price? Incidentally, you must not be so extravagant though it is sweet and generous of you to want to spend so much on us. But we quite realise the pinch you must be feeling at home.

Show this letter to Mummy, won't you, and thank her for the duckstone,
My love to all.

Your affectionate sister,
Mary.

Shore's Hotel,
Napier Road,
Rawalpindi.

4th Feb. 1940.

My dear Mummy,

It's simply ages since I've written, I know, but,
oh, dear, what a time we've been having! You'll be
getting tired of letters that start like that! Harry
has been in hospital again, this time with pleurisy –
they think they let him out too soon after the 'flu.
Luckily he didn't get it badly, and they say the patch
on his lungs is now quite healed up, but it was nasty
while it lasted, and it was awful to hear his breathing.
He has just come out of hospital again, with strict
injunctions to take things very easily indeed, and has
been told he is unfit for active service for a month,
which may mean he'll be down here for the month. You
see, if they say he can return for light office duty,
Harry can tell them there isn't such a thing in Wana,
if he goes back to Wana, he's got to take his part in
columns and so on, and of course he won't be fit for
that till the month is over. Isn't it a pity it can't
be extended over March as well, so that he'll be here for
the great event!

They say troubles never come singly, and I really
haven't liked to write to you because I'm afraid I have
some very disappointing news for you. Your coat has not
yet been sent off! I really thought it had been, when I
wrote and told you so, but we hadn't arranged with the shop
that they should do the packing as they could naturally do
it better than we could, and attend to the insurance, etc.,
simply sending us the bill. We had already given a cheque
towards the cost of the coat. Well, the shop held the
parcel up because of some difficulty over the insurance –
it was more expensive than we had reckoned on, and they
wanted to ask us about it, you see – and in the meantime
it had been discovered that Harry had been overpaid on
his three months' leave in Kashmir to the tune of Rs.1,000
which was promptly deducted from his pay at the rate of
a third of his pay every month – an absolutely crippling
amount! So we had to cancel the cheque to the furriers
and we haven't yet been able to pay for the coat, and of
course they won't post it until they've at least got a
substantial deposit.

No wonder we thought we were so rich on
that three months leave. Army pay is so complicated with its
allowances and deductions that only a babu could work it
out, and this time one of them had made a mistake.   He
had forgotten to deduct income tax, had given us separation
allowance, and had forgotten various other deductions.
Rˢ.1,000 is no mean sum to pay off, and our finances are in
a state of utter chaos - you see, having the money we
naturally thought we were rich and spent it!   I feel
awful every time I hear on the wireless what bitter weather
you are having, and think how much you must be wanting your
fur, but what could we do about it?   We hope to send it
this month, though, if the bank can be persuaded to let us
have an overdraft - they've been a bit sticky about it so
far.   So you may get it in time to wear on cold summer
evenings!   Oh, dear, it is so disappointing;   it would
have been so nice for you this winter,

        I had been worrying about what I was going to do when
Harry returned to Wana, as I obviously couldn't be left by
myself at such a late stage, but that difficulty has been
solved because Vivian and Louise Smith have asked me to go
and stay with them as soon as Harry goes back.   They have
a car, so they can take me down to the hospital when
necessary.   Louise is an awfully nice girl, I've played
mah-johngg with her a lot.   They're newly-weds.

        Betty Barham has gone up to Bannu.   Her husband was
suddenly transferred there about a fortnight ago.   I miss
her a lot.

        Preparations for the son-and-heir or daughter-and-
disappointment are progressing apace.   We've got a nice
sturdy little second-hand cot, which we have painted white,
and a beautiful little secondhand kerosene stove, dirt
cheap in the khabari bazaar, for cooking the baby's food,
boiling its milk, etc.   I don't see why I shouldn't also
use it for more interesting things like toffee and fudge,
so do please send me your recipe for fudge-making, as I've
never tasted any as good as yours.   And do please send
the things for the baby quickly, as things may take up to
six weeks to come out, and its due in two months!   I've
knitted a couple of blankets, crochetted a shawl, knitted
little coats and bootees, and made some Viyella frocks -
very odd-looking they are too, I seem to have got half the
seams the wrong way round, and they all look lop-sided,
somehow.   But alone I did them - and if the infant doesn't
like them, it knows what it can do about it.

- 3 -

I don't think there is any other news, except that
it has been raining for the last fortnight, and we're jolly
glad of it after so many months of dust. Also a girl
called Pat McCaulay who knows how to smock, has promised
me a blue chepe-de-chine smock for the infant, which I
think is very sweet of her.

Much love to all of you.

Your loving daughter,

Mary

Shore's Hotel,
Napier Rd,
R: Pindi.
22nd Feb '40

My dear Flip,

Thanks for your letters, which arrived close to each other. You <u>are</u> a mug getting German measles at your age, but I expect Mummy was thankful, as it enabled her to get coal on a doctor's certificate! Please assure Mummy that I <u>have</u> written several times since I told her about my illness — naturally I have, since I realised she would probably be a bit anxious about me at such a time. There was a gap when Harry was ill for the second time, but I wrote airmail after that to make up for it. Harry was given a month's sick leave by the medical board, so he will be here till the middle of March and then what happens to him, we don't know. Doesn't it seem a pity, though, that his leave should end a fortnight before the great event, as he will probably have to return to Wana, and goodness knows how long it will be before he sees the   .

2.

You said in one letter that there were a lot of questions you wanted to ask me, but you didn't like to. Well, don't be silly, but ask away. If only women weren't so ignorant about such an important matter, they wouldn't be so nervous about it. I always thought one was sick for the whole nine months! whereas I know now that one is only sick just at the beginning, and then only a little, sometimes it's nothing worse than a slight attack of nausea. Then at about three months, you get what feels like indigestion. That stage soon passes, and for the rest of the time you feel grand — I don't mean just not ill, but positively and gloriously well. The great idea is to keep the baby as small as possible, so you must cut down meat, particularly beef — never eat meat more than once in the day, and not at all towards the end. And you must <u>not</u> lie on a sofa and look pale and interesting, but take as much exercise as possible without getting overtired. Nothing violent, of course. I can't play golf any more, because my tummy gets in the way of the swing! but I do a

3.

lot of walking. Another thing I had dreaded was the tedium of the long wait, but believe me, every moment of it is fun, there is so much to do and plan. Choosing your patterns, buying your materials and wools, and the actual knitting, sewing and embroidery — these keep you too busy to be bored and baby things are so pretty and fascinating to make. I have been lent a sewing-machine, and I have actually cut out and made some little frocks and nighties all by myself! I have had to make thin things for the first month of its life — April — and then warm things for Murree, so it has been little muslin nighties and slightly larger Viyella ones. Embroidered with feather-stitching! It's amazing the number of presents one receives for a first baby. Pat McCaulay is making it a smock, Pat Davies has promised me a brush-and-comb set, Norah Foss has given me three pairs of bootees and Marjorie Williams has given me three knitted coats and three knitted vests.

Talking about Marjorie (the Deputy Commissioner's wife), I met a young I.C.S. lad at her house a little while ago, and

4.

was able to have a good long talk with him. He is pretty sure that I *am* entitled to that dowry, but he says you can only find out for certain from India House. He also says Mummy can soon settle any doubts as to whether she will receive a pension or not on Daddy's death, by asking at India House, as he says there are definite rules about that kind of thing, worked out to the third and fourth wife in divorce cases !! He suggests that you ask to see a Mr. George Anderson, & mention his name – Clinton Thomas. He says even if it is not in Mr. Anderson's province, he will be able to direct you to the right department.

Show Mummy this page because this is all very important.

We were absolutely horrified to hear that Mummy was given no money at all for January and only £10 for February. How can she be expected to live? Daddy cannot legally stop her alimony, and Uncle Dick's behaviour as her lawyer is little short of criminal. She says in

5.

her letter she doesn't want to offend him or Auntie Dot, but surely she must realise that avoiding giving offence to Auntie Dot by keeping Uncle Dick as her lawyer is proving a very expensive luxury, in fact one that she cannot afford! Uncle Dick has done her down a good many times now. Tell Mummy to do this (for goodness' sake, show her this, so that she can see how much in earnest I am about it):— to go to the Bank, see the manager (and no one else) and put the whole matter before him, asking him if the Bank's legal department would help her. (Every bank has its own legal department). I'm pretty sure she will find that they will be willing to advise her free or for a very small charge (she can find out from the manager) & will very likely undertake to fight her case. I don't know about the Westminster, but Lloyds' bank has a legal department that will undertake work for the bank's customers, so it would be worth Mummy's while to see the manager and find out —

6.

It is most unfortunate that all this should have happened at a time when we cannot possibly send Mummy any money because we are in debt ourselves, owing to the Unit Accountant's mistake over our advance of pay for leave. (I explained all this in my last letter to Mummy). Harry has been obliged temporarily to stop the monthly allowance to his mother.

<u>What</u> a life! What wouldn't I do for £100, or even Rs. 100/- !!!

The Barhams are coming back to Pindi. John has been posted to the M.T.T. Battn. here, which means a cushy job in a family station for the next four years. Several R.I.A.S.C. people here are hopping mad with rage about it, because John has just come back from 18 months at home, and his "Frontier tour" since he came back has consisted of six weeks in Bannu - a family station! Whereas there are people who <u>do</u> deserve a cushy job, one man, for example, who is now doing his 6th year on the frontier in the last eight years! John was posted to Razmak originally, but that was changed to Bannu on the plea

7.

that he was married !!!! No-one held Harry's hand when he was posted to Wana and said "There, there, he shan't go, he's married!" And we'd been married a much shorter time then than the Barhams. And the man who has done six years in eight on the frontier is also married! Can you wonder that they're short of officers in the R.I.A.S.C., when it seems to be run on favouritism?

At the same time for selfish reasons I'm glad, because it will be so nice to have Betty Barham here again!

Forgive the outburst, pudden-face. Remember that you must take care of yourself as an expectant aunt!

Much love to you and all.

Your loving sister,

Mary.

5 Willcocks Road
Peshawar
NWFP

16th March 1940

My dear Mummy,

Just take a careful look at the address! And you
can't be more surprised than we are, we were only told
to move to Peshawar three days ago, and arrived last
night. We had known for some time that Harry' company
was moving here, but had been given to understand that he
would not move with his company as he had not finished
his two years on the frontier, so this is an amazing bit of
luck. Would you believe it, we only received our orders
to move here at 6.30pm on the day that Harry was going to
catch the 9.20pm train on his way back to Wana, only three
hours before he was due to leave, in fact. Actually the
company doesn't arrive here for a few days and Harry is
now on an extension of leave, but we had to make the move
while it was still safe for me to travel, the infant is due
in ten days!

What thrills us so particularly is that at long
last we have our own bungalow. A most palatial one it is
too, colossal rooms with ceiling fans in most of them, and
deep verahdahs back and front so it should be beautifully
cool during the hot weather, and I don't think it will be
necessary for me to go to the hills for very long. In Pindi
there were no such things as ceiling fans and the rooms
were nearly all very small so it soon became unbearable.

We arrived about eight yesterday evening,
having sent the bearer ayah and cook in advance with
instructions to hire enough furniture for the night,
and get as much ready as possible, anyway, clean out the

bungalow, as it had been unoccupied for some time. When we arrived we set to work to unpack the glass and china until we had enough for dinner that night and breakfast the next morning. It was a thrill to use for the first time the lovely dinner set that Phyllis gave us! We have finished unpacking that particular box now, and have really been extraordinarily lucky. Phyllis' dinner set has no breakages, the cream coloured breakfast set is also entire, the tea set from James (which was there after all!) has only one cup broken and that not badly, I think it can be mended. Among the Woolworth stuff only two glasses were broken, which doesn't matter very much. The glass from Bulge is ok, in fact the only tragedy is Harry' willow pattern Toby jug. It remains to be seen how the stuff from Calcutta survives the journey here.

We spent most of this morning choosing furniture. We are furnishing as sparsely as possible as the stuff is on hire at so much per article per month. The bungalow is too big for us to furnish all the rooms, as for the number of windows and doors to be curtained –! Luckily the previous occupants also had economical ideas and white washed the bathroom windows so they don't need curtains, and as the hot weather is coming on I shan't curtain the doors. There is a huge square hall which is really meant to be the drawing room, but we are leaving it as a hall and using a smaller but prettier room with a bow window looking onto the prettiest bit of the garden. The garden is lovely. A lawn in front and a long narrow lawn down each side with beds stiff with double stock and heliotrope. There is also a bed of antirrhinums, another with pansies and double daisies (I don't know what a gardener would call them!). Also carnations, freesias, hollyhocks and poppies, and several rose bushes, but these are only in bed at the moment. A kitchen garden with tomatoes and lettuce two fig trees (nearly ripe) and three orange trees (second crop no in bud). And a lime tree with ripe fruit. Peshawar is a pretty place much greener than Pindi. The lawns are real lawns not mere patches of brown earth as they are in Pindi.

We have just had a visit from KC Khanna, a friend from Murree and Srinagar days, whose regiment is stationed here. We phoned his mess to tell him of our arrival and he came round directly he got the message, but alas! He is off to the frontier on Monday. He was delighted with our transfer, and doesn't expect to be on the frontier very long. We shan't be lonely anyway, as we have a very cordial invitation from KC's family to go round there at any time. They are coming to see us when we are settled in. Also Harry has discovered two old friends of his here, one he knew in Calcutta and one he knew in Fort Sandeman, both married.

The Barhams are coming to stay with us for Easter. They arrived back in Pindi about a week before we left. Betty is a dear she has given me the sweetest little frock for the baby, also three pairs of bootees and a baby basket.

The financial situation has now eased a trifle, and we have been able at long last to get your coat. The shop packed it in front of us, but we decided we'd better post it ourselves, remembering what happened last time, we thought it was well on its way when they suddenly sprung it on us it hadn't gone at all. There should be no duty to pay, as we had it lined with satin instead of silk on purpose.

18th March.

Oh dear, what a business it is getting settled into a bungalow, measuring up for curtains and chair covers, matting for the floor and chicks for the verandah, and then dashing round choosing materials. We have got Bokhara silk for the drawing room curtains, as it is very cheap and looks cool and pretty. We have got one shot with green and a dullish pink, and the chair covers are cream coloured with a green pattern which picks out the green of the curtains.

Dealing with the cook is a bit of a business, as it has to be done in my rather limited Urdu (the ayah also speaks no English). However, I'm managing pretty well. He does make some comic mistakes though. Yesterday we had KC to dinner, for which I had ordered tomato soup, mutton with mint sauce, etc. chocolate soufflé, angles on horseback. He seemed a little vague about the last item, so I explained, a prune wrapped up in bacon on toast. All went well, the soufflé was a dream, until the arrival of a very odd looking savoury, he used prawns instead of prunes! It tasted pretty good though. Harry, you will probably remember, won't eat any sweet, so I ordered cheese soufflé to follow the meat tonight, we got a weird mixture of cheese and fish, goodness knows why fish. But it all adds to the general fun!

The ayah came in today looking very pleased with herself and presented me with some bright yellow socks she had knitted for the infant, I suppose the poor thing will have to wear them or she'll be offended!

Do you remember sending me a photograph of yourself a goodish time back? Harry has cut it out from the background, and put it in a glass frame, you know the kind, you put the photo between two sheets of glass, and it does look nice. It occupies a proud position on the drawing room mantel piece.

Well, if the infant's reasonably punctual, I should have some interesting news in my next letter, of course we'll send you a cable at the time, though.

Much love to you all, your very loving daughter.
Mary.

5, Willcocks Road,
Peshawar,
N.W.F.P.

29th March '40.

My dear Flip,

    The wretched little brat is taking after its father and being unpunctual. It's already three days late. Not that I'm worried, because I know the calculated date is liable to be a fortnight out either way, but I'm getting very impatient to know whether it's a boy or a girl and what it looks like!

    You have got a genius for having an awful time, haven't you? Tonsils would be quite enough for most people, without following them up with German measles, an assortment of boils, and an abscess in the ear. Is that enough for the time being, or have you thought out any other amusements in the meantime?

    A letter has just this minute arrived, explaining about the income-tax and about the dowry. So after all Daddy isn't doing Mummy down, though after past behaviour he can hardly be surprised if we don't trust him an inch, and I must say I was all het up for battle on Mummy's behalf. Too bad about the dowry, but then I always had a feeling it was rather too good to be true!

    Running a bungalow is the grandest fun, and my Urdu is improving rapidly. I have to speak it to the cook, though he gets his accounts written in English of a sort. Of a sort! I was considerably startled at being charged 5 annas for "tall fate" the other day. We argued about it for nearly twenty minutes, and eventually I had to appeal to Harry for help. It turned out to be "tail fat", in other words, lard. (From the fat-tailed sheep you get up here). He kept saying something about "tail", but then "tail" is the Urdu for oil, so I kept arguing that we already had enough and he shouldn't have bought any more, so we were at completely cross purposes. I must say housekeeping out here is a very different matter, the more finicky and troublesome the dish you order, the better pleased the cook seems to be! Now that Harry's company has arrived, we get fresh vegetables from the Company garden twice a week which all helps.

- 2 -

Harry's company arrived in two batches, which
meant getting up twice at 6 a.m. to meet them
at the station.   Harry told me that though
it was not exactly expected of me to go too, it would be
appreciated if I did, so I went, and the appreciation took
the form of bouquets of sweet-peas and marigolds;   it would
take an Indian to think out such a combination!   And then
I had to go down to the lines, and try to make intelligent
remarks about the mules;   during which time a sepoy
followed me around holding an umbrella over my head;   it
was a cloudy day, but not raining, so I don't know what
it was for;   just in case, I suppose!

The Company owns a tonga drawn by two fat mules,
which is at my disposal whenever I want to go out for
shopping or anything else.   Also uniformed driver;   in
fact, an impsoing equipage!   The first time I used it,
I had a grinning little Kamauni also in attendance, who
followed me from counter to counter and collected the
parcels.   I didn't mind him standing by while I selected
cheese and coffee;   but I could <u>not</u> get rid of him when I
went into a chemist's to do some rather intimate shopping;
no, he'd been told to carry the Memsahib's parcels, and the
Memsahib's parcels he was going to carry.   In desperation
I bought some soap I didn't want, and told Harry I didn't
really need anyone to go round with me.   Next day I
shopped in peace.

I don't agree at all with this idea of inducing the
baby a fortnight early.   Remember the calculated date may
be a fortnight out <u>either way</u>, so you might induce the poor
thing a <u>month</u> early!   Premature birth is a very great shock
to the baby, and it is liable to arrive incomplete - minus
finger-nails, etc.   They'd grow later, of course;   but
what is the point of inducing it early?   Really, Nature
<u>does</u> know best!

Our pride and joy here is the garden;   the lawn is a
real lawn, richly green, quite unlike the bare brown
patches that were called lawns in Pindi;   and the flower-
beds are a thick mass of stock, antirrhimums, hollyhocks,
and goodness knows what;   the roses are just beginning,
and the orange-trees are a mass of blossom.   Peshawar is
a heavenly place.

- 3 -

Well, I must now make out some menus for Harry
for when I am in hospital, otherwise, he'll
probably order roast mutton every day because
he can't be bothered to think out anything else!
Incidentally, I'm extremely pleased with myself
for discovering two puddings that he will eat - and with
relish; ginger snaps and cocoanut pancakes, both of which
the cook makes to perfection.

Would you have believed that I <u>could</u> get so domesticated!

<u>British ~~Families Hospital~~</u>
An hour after this was written, I was
whisked off to hospital! where I was
promptly given a very hot ~~bath~~ and told to
walk about to bring on the pains faster.
I had a distinctly uncomfortable night
but the pains didn't get really bad
till morning. I went into the delivery
room at 11 o'clock and young Anthony arrived
at 4.45 that afternoon. I was conscious the
whole time, they only gave me a couple of
whiffs of chloroform at the end, & then
not enough to put me out. And I'm <u>very</u>
proud of the fact that I only screamed
twice at the end, though I did make
some moany noises. The doctor was very
pleased, because he said ~~the~~ it made such
a difference if the patient didn't

4.

make a fuss, and I really had quite a bad time as the little blighter arrived all cock-eyed. The doctor said arriving head-first was the only natural thing he did! Oh, but it was so marvellous afterwards! The doctor and nurse went away for a few minutes, leaving me on the delivery table & the baby wrapped up in a cot waiting for its first bath. And he talked to me, I swear he did! I kept saying "Uh-huh" to him & he always answered "Uh-huh!"

Believe me, "in labour" is no empty phrase; you have to make the effort yourself to push the baby through, no one can help you with that, & jolly hard work it is. And yet it's surprising how little you feel it afterwards, I'm positive I could have walked back to my room if I'd been allowed to.

If only you were all here, I do so want to show off my beautiful baby! He is beautiful, I'm not just being a prejudiced mother, he was born with an unusual amount

5.

of hair, fine & silky & golden, which of course helps his appearance a lot. He isn't red & crinkly, like most new babies, but pink-&-white & chubby, with lovely blue eyes. His eyes, we think, will be like mine, but his nose like Harry's. His mouth is a little difficult to tell at the moment. When he's feeding he looks like a little pink fish - you know what a goldfish's mouth looks like when it's feeding?

Do you know, I'm so hale & hearty after it, that I'm allowed other visitors besides Harry on the ~~third~~ day!

Harry is sweet with it, & simply adores it. When he comes to see me, he keeps walking over to the cot for another peep, & then comes back grinning from ear to ear. Of course I've done the right thing in having a boy; the Company are delighted.

I'm now wondering how soon we can afford to have another — !!

Much love, Auntie!

Mary

British Families Hospital.
Peshawar.
5th April, 1940.

My dear Mummy,

We were so pleased with your cable, and your message was duly passed on to young Anthony, who, I regret to say, received it with an air of boredom! Isn't it all thrilling, we are so frightfully pleased because it is a boy. Next time I shall want a girl, but I did so hope this one would be a boy.

Well, it wasn't so bad, though the doctor said it wasn't frightfully easy, as the little blighter arrived back to front, in fact the doctor said, arriving head-first was the only natural thing he did do. I was conscious the whole time, they gave me chloroform at the end, but not enough to put me right out. But I only screamed twice! Wasn't that good?

2.

It was rather funny just afterwards, because of course I asked what it was the moment it was taken away, and the doctor said "a girl." I was so disappointed, and said "Well, we'll have to have another." A few minutes later he said "I seem to have made a mistake, it's a boy after all." But I wouldn't believe it till I'd seen for myself!

He's a lovely baby, and that's not just the inevitable remark of the proud mamma. He is lovely. He was born with an unusual amount of hair, so soft and silky and golden, he has very good features, and is beautifully pink and white and chubby, not red and crinkly like most new babies. I have lots of milk for him, and he guzzles like billy-oh; he is flourishing as you can realise when I tell you that at six days' old he is only 1 oz. under birth-weight!

He is definitely going to be more like Harry than me. His little snub nose is going to be like Harry's, you can tell

9.

by the nostrils. And his mouth is absurdly like Harry's. He is such a funny little bundle, don't babies have a priceless variety of expressions, mostly such solemn ones! And what an extraordinary amount of character they have, even on the first day! Well, you can be proud of your grandson. We'll send you a snap of him as soon as possible. Harry is a very proud papa!

The proud mother is sitting up in bed, plump & pink-cheeked, & bursting to be up and about. However, this doctor (who is awfully nice, a Capt. Newton) is stricter with flourishing mothers than with mothers who are ill, as he says the flourishing ones try to do too much, so I'm afraid I won't be let loose till the full fortnight is over.

Isn't it grand to have a flat tummy again? But oh dear, my matronly bosom —!

With fondest love from both of us and "love to Granny from Anthony."

Your loving daughter,
Mary.

5, Willcocks Road,
Peshawar.
13th April 1940.

Darling Mummy,

Thanks so much for your lovely letter, which only took ten
days to get here, and arrived the day before I left hospital.
I came out yesterday morning, and you can imagine the thrill of
taking young Anthony home; all the servants crowding round to see
him and the dogs wild with excitement, and, to my great relief,
not the least bit jealous.   I can't believe that he only arrived
a fortnight ago; every time I look at him, I think: "I can't
possibly have produced that!"   He was weighed yesterday and is
7 lbs. 12 oz., which is 8 oz. over birthweight; pretty good
going in a fortnight!   Incidentally, Harry made a mistake in the
cable; he told me he had cabled the weight as 7¾lbs. whereas it
should have been 7¼lbs.   The Saturday night on which he arrived
Harry went out to celebrate, and got so bottled that he went round
the club telling people that his wife had just produced a 9¼lbs.
baby, and it was a record for the hospital; as a result of which
I had a stream of people poking their noses round my door and
asking if they might see the record baby!

It was sweet of you to send that cable when you are so hard up,
and it was much appreciated.   The baby clothes have not arrived,
instead I got a notification from London that they could not be
sent to me as there was no Customs declaration form with them,
therefore would I write back telling them the name of the sender
to whom they must be returned.   Isn't it infuriating, especially
after you had taken the trouble to make enquiries and find out that
there was no Customs Duty on them.   I shall reply to the Authorities
concerned by airmail (they wrote sea-mail to me, so I have only just
received their letter!).   Then when you have got the parcel back,
it will take another month for it to get here!   I suggest that you
leave out any very tiny garments as it will be too late for first-
size things by then, but anything a bit larger would be welcome.
The delay is so disappointing, I can remember the dainty things
Angela used to wear, and was longing to see little Anthony in them.
Yes, you are quite right about the long clothes, the modern idea is
to leave the legs free to kick.   But it's a very easy matter to
shorten little frocks.

Anthony is such a good baby; he sleeps from one feed-time to
the next, and only cries when he is being changed, which he doesn't
like.   He adores his bath; if only you could see him in it,
looking like a little pink frog, and with the most blissful
expression on his face.   Everybody falls in love with him, the
night-sister was so fond of him that she knitted him a little blue
coat, and almost wept when she said good-bye.   She is an awfully
nice girl, so I've asked her to come round and see him sometimes.
And when she does, won't I just crow over her, because she said
that babies always cried the first few nights at home, because of

2.

the strangeness, but Anthhny never made a sound last night! (It is nice to have someone to whom I can pour out my raptures without being afraid of being a bore!)

I don't know if I mentioned in any previous letters that we had come across a good lady here whom we met in Srinagar last year? She is a Mrs. Hodgins, a widow with a grown-up daughter called Adza. They have been so kind to us; when I was in hospital the old girl took Harry under her wing, and was always asking him to lunch or dinner, so that he shouldn't be lonely, and they called in their car to take me away from hospital. I was so pleased to have my little man to myself at last, that I would scarcely let the ayah touch him, I insisted on bathing and changing himsmyself. To-day the ayah is being allowed to change him, because I found it so tiring!

Yesterday evening we went rouhd to see the Hodgins and thanked them for their kindness, and then went to see the Mewtons, with whom Harry had made friends while I was in hospital. (Capt.Mewton was the doctor who attended me; he is a famous gynaecologist). I hadn't met Mrs. Mewton before; she is every bit as nice as he is, and promised to ask mē round one morning so that I could meet some of the other wives. They are both mad keen on riding (he is tiny enough for a jockey), and she said that as soon as I was able to start riding, she was sure her husband would give me some lessons (I explained I hadn't ridden since Calcutta and was afraid I'd forgotten everything), and then she would come out with me till I had sufficient experience and confidence to go out alone. Wasn't that extraordinarily sweet and kind of her, I do hope she means it. I think she does, because Harry was able to help her husband; he wanted to buy a certain buggy (people still drive about in buggies here!!) and was asked Rs.200 for it; Harry sent one of his Indian officers to buy the buggy, and being an Indian he managed to get it for only ₨100 - exactly half-price! And of course he was delighted.

There is also another couple here we know; Harry had known the husband in Calcutta, and I had met the wife in Murree! Their name is Roe. They came round to see me in hospital several times and sent me masses of flowers and magazines. They are a nice couple and very cheery, but they are always on the razzle-dazzle, we can't hope to keep up with them, and they are two of the hardest drinkers I've ever met; so in spite of their friendliness and the fact that they are so likable, I'm afraid we'll have to avoid getting too friendly with them. Harry agrees with me.

Anyway, we've got a good start in Peshawar by knowing these people, and by the time we've made all the necessary calls, we should know masses of people. And now I'm back, the round of calls must begin. I should imagine Pehsawar has altered perhaps the least of all the places you knew; the club is still famous

3.

for its jolly friendly atmosphere; and there are still dog-roses
in the hedges!   I have fallen in love with Peshawar, little
though I have seen of it.

Auntie Bar's bed-jcket, I regret to say, has not yet arrived,
but for goodness' sake don't tell her that; say that I was
delighted with it, and she should get a letter from me very shortly.
I will write directly it arrives, but I must wait till then so that
I can make suitable comments!

I described Anthony to you in the first letter I wrote after
the event; now that he's a little older, I can only add that he
looks more like Harry than ever!   The first comment everyone
makes on him is always: "But how ridiculously like Harry!"   In
spite of which he is a remarkably pretty baby!!   But I think he
is going to have my eyes; his eyes are already a little darker,
and are obviously not going to stay blue.   But there, you shall
have snapshots as soon as possible.

Thank Phyllis and Angela very much for their letters, which
will be answered with all possible speed.   Angela is not to
forget she is a godmother as well as an aunt!   I shall have to
find someone here to be "proxy" for her.

With much love to you all,

from all three of us!

Your loving daughter,

Mary

5, Willcocks Road,
Peshawar, N.W.F.P.

2nd May, 1940.

My dear Angela,

This is to wish you many happy returns of your birthday, and
to tell you that you are now a godmother!

Your godson and nephew disgraced himself at the christening
by yelling the place down, and really I'm not surprised - the
things they did to the poor little man - !   He had oil rubbed on
his chest and on his back, on his forehead and on the back of his
head, salt in his mouth, and of course water poured over his head.
Each fresh indignity was greeted with shrieks of protest.   The
only thing that kept him quiet for a bit was the salt.   You could
see him thinking: "Gosh! something to eat!   Can there be more to
follow - ?"   He was christened Anthony Edward Richard.   Harry
suddenly inserted the Edward at the last moment, because he said
his family always had an Edward.

There were quite a few people at the christening, considering
how short a time we have been in Peshawar.   These dispersed after
the ceremony and assembled at the bungalow later for a little drink
party.   Some of them brought presents.   Col. & Mrs. Hickie, who
stood proxy for the godparents, gave young Tony a beer-tankard with
his initials on it; Col. Masters, a Parsee doctor whom Harry had
known in Wana, gave a silver porridge dish, a small one, and a spoon;
Major & Mrs. Milne brought a rattle composed of a silver elephant
with two little bells attached, hanging from an ivory ring;   The
Roes brought a pretty little smock, embroidered with little boys
chasing big red butterflies!

The little man is flourishing; although only a month old, he
is two pounds over birth-weight.   This won't mean anything to you,
but tell Mummy, and see if she isn't impressed!   We have taken two
snaps of him, which unfortunately have not come out very well, but
we will send them; they will come by sea-mail, though, because of
the weight. (Sea-mail is going round the Cape now, so goodness
knows how long it will take.)   Young Tony would go to sleep when
we were taking his photograph; the camera bored him to tears, the
little wretch.   He is a source of constant interest to the dogs,
and there is always one on duty by his cot; only known and
privileged persons dare approach that cot!   Incidentally we now
have three dogs, having acquired an attractive but brainless
Dalmatian.

Peshawar appears to be suffering from a plague of scorpions
at the moment - beastly things!   They are always dropping from
the ceilings, and the ayah was so badly stung that she was laid up
for the rest of that day and the whole of the next day.   And as

for the centipedes - ! You just wouldn't believe the size they grow to; Harry killed one in the bedroom the other day that was nine inches long, and horribly thick in the body, too. He said he'd never seen anything like it, even in the hills. We had been having drinks with the Roes, and when I saw that centipede I thought the Roes must have been putting gin in my orange squashes!

You appear to be a reformed character! Mummy's and Phyllis' letters are full of how hard you are working for your exam. You _must_ get honours in that exam., Phyllis and I both did, so don't let the family down! But I expect you'll do better than either of us did.

Does the war make things very dull for you? It is so difficult for us out here to imagine what it really is like for you at home. It is difficult to realise the actuality of the Norwegian invasion; we always listen to the news on the wireless, but somehow it seems unreal, like some fantastic novel by H.G.Wells. People out here are lucky. I wish I could transport the whole bunch of you to Peshawar!

Peshawar is much cooler than Pindi; we have only just begun to use fans. I shan't go up to Murree till June 3rd, when Harry hopes to be able to get ten days' leave to take me up there. My address will be: The Viewforth Hotel, Murree, Punjab. You had all better address your letters there in future, as I shall be there by the time the letters reache India.

My love to Mummy and Phyllis, and tell them not to be alarmed if there is a gap in letters, because this going round the Cape business is going to make them take longer.

> With lots of love,
> from your loving sister,
>
> Mary.

P.S. We have had a storm in which it rained mud !!

The Viewforth Hotel,
Murree.

14th June, 1940.

Darling Mummy,

Your last letter made me feel I could cheerfully wring
Daddy's neck.   I don't believe anyone could be beastlier
than he.   How can he expect you to live on £10 for two
months, and the prospect of getting more "when he can manage
it"?   And just now, too, when everything must be getting so
much more expensive.   It drives me nearly crazy that we
can't help.   But we are getting clear gradually, and in a
few months I really believe we could send you something, just
a little now and then to help you out.   I have never let
Daddy know about the baby, I don't feel I want to have anything at all to do with him.   Incidentally, why do you go
on sticking to Uncle Dick, I'm positive he's doing you down;
at any rate he is no help.   For heaven's sake get a decent
lawyer.   I'm sure Uncle Dick's management of the case would
not bear investigation.   That's Harry's opinion.

Well, we've got some news too, which is not so good.
We came up here about a week ago; Harry got ten days' leave
to bring me up.   We were here only three days when Harry
received orders to go to Ambala.   He had to be in Ambala
at the end of his leave, so we had to dash down to Peshawar
again and pack up the bungalow.   What a business - and just
to help matters the bearer got fever and didn't do a scrap of
the packing.   When we left Peshawar it was 118° in the shade
and not a bit funny, but luckily by the time we had returned
from Murree there had been a storm which cooled things down
a bit.   The baby didn't seem to mind, he likes the heat and
adores the car.   Harry couldn't have got to Ambala in time
by car, so he left that in a garage in Peshawar and we went
by train.   When we reached ~~Peshawar~~ Pindi, the baby and I
were pushed out on to the platform to take a taxi up the hill
while Harry went on to Ambala.

The drive up was a nightmare, with an Indian driver whose
one idea seemed to be to get there as fast as the car would go.
You know that dreadful winding road full of hairpin bends and
with a sheer drop on one side!   Well, he took those corners

- 2 -

on two wheels - just whizzed round them- till
I hit on the bright idea of telling him if he
went so fast round corners the baby would be
sick.   After that he went slowly enough, but
turned round at every corner to ask if the baby were all
right!   I told him I would look after the baby if he would
be good enough to keep his eyes on the road.   However, in
spite of these alarms we arrived without mishap.   Murree
is quite hot, which is a good thing as it is not too sudden
a change for young Tony.

If only you could see him now!   he plays with his
fingers and gurgles and smiles in the most delicious manner.
He is very pale, poor little mite, after that dreadful
heat, but quite well and happy, and he'll soon get roses
up here.   I enclose some snaps that have been taken at
different times, but I have written his age at the back
of them.   Betty Barham has taken some snaps of us together
with our babies, and the two ayahs with the babies.   Hers
is now a year old - a little girl.   I'll send these as
soon as I can get the prints.

I told you in one of my letters that I was going to
stay with Betty in her bungalow out at Kuldana, but I can't
after all, as they are rather short of quarters in Kuldana
and the spare part of her bungalow, which I was to occupy,
has been taken over by some Major.   It does seem a pity,
anyway, it is nice to have her up here, ad I know I can go
there whenever I like.   There are a lot of people here I
know, grass-widows from Pindi, mostly!

Murree is full of babies, I peep into all the prams
when I go out, but I haven't yet seen a baby nearly as nice
as mine!

I have had a letter from Phyllis telling me about her
efforts to get a better job, and of her move up to Hatfield
to work with De Havillands.   It is enterprising of her,
and plucky, I think, as she thought she would know nobody
there.   I'm glad that she has found friends after all.

I don't know where you are now, as you say in your
letter you are going to stay with Auntie May, and I don't
know her address.   So I shall send this to he Bracken to
be forwarded.

- 3 -

I don't blame you for leaving the Bracken,
Auntie Dot is a kindly old soul and means well
enough, but for ill-mannered loutishness,
recommend me Boots, Blighty, Pie and Pooh.
And they are <u>so</u> little-minded.

The war news is too awful, I'm thankful I'm out here -
wish I could transport all of you out here too! Isn't it
odd how my history seems to be following yours? - I mean
my position now is much the same as yours during the last
war. Only I've got a very different kind of husband,
thank heaven. Poor Mummy. Never mind, keep cheerful
and remember that we'll send what help we can as soon as
we are able.

Lots of love from
your loving daughter,

Mary

Cecil Hotel,
Ambala.
26th June '40.

My dear Flip,

There's a surprise address for you! Not a pleasant surprise from my point of view — Ambala is a God-forsaken spot on the borders of the Punjab near the U.P. — strikingly, swelteringly hot. But you will be wanting to know how we got here. We went up to Murree at the beginning of this month. Peshawar was 118° and we were glad to leave it. Harry had ten days leave to take me up there, and we'd planned all sorts of dances and picnics with John & Betty Barham during these ten days. The first two days were wet, but we enjoyed them and went to one cocktail dance. On the afternoon of the third day Harry got a wire recalling him as he had been posted to Ambala and had to hand over his company in Peshawar first. I had to go too, in order to pack up everything in the bungalow. We had three foully hot days in Peshawar, and I had to do every scrap of the packing myself, because the old bearer got fever!

There was hardly any time to make proper arrangements, for instance, we had no time to

2.

sell the car, we had to hand it over to a garage to sell for us — a most unsatisfactory arrangement. Then we got on to the Ambala train. When we reached Pindi at 8 p.m., the baby, ayah & myself & Peter, the bull-terrier (the other two dogs, Buttons & Becky were being looked after by Betty Barham, alias "Bees'knees", in Murree), disembarked, said goodbye to Harry, spent the night in stifling Pindi, & took a taxi up the hill the next morning. Wasn't I thankful to reach Murree again, with its delicious cool breeze off the distant snows!

Beesknees was living in Kuldana, about three miles out of Murree — a lovely walk. I used to go and see her a lot, or she would come up to Murree & we would have a coffee at the club. Or I would take little Tony out in his pram, which he loved, & of course we hadn't been able to use it down in the plains. I went to two dances, both times with a Col Shelton — a dirty old man, I strongly suspected. I insisted on going home by myself in a single rickshaw — rather funny — "Oh, no, Trevor, you _really_ mustn't bother — couldn't _dream_ of

3.

letting you come all that way — miles out
of your way! — " etc. Only trouble
was, I then had to pay for the rickshaw!
I had to give to bull-terrier away, which
nearly broke my heart, he was a magnificent animal,
but he and Buttons couldn't stand each other, &
I couldn't stand a series of dog-fights! I gave
him to a girl called Beryl Roe from Peshawar.
She loved him, but he attacked and bit all her
boy-friends when they called to take her out!
However, she kept him.

Into this pleasant life of walks among pine
trees with magnificent scenery to look at, mah-johngg,
and pleasant chatter with the many old friends from
Pindi, and occasional dances, Harry's wire came
like a bombshell. He told me to leave for Ambala
at once. I turned quite cold and felt sick.
I didn't know what on earth it meant, and it
was a beastly journey for the unfortunate baby at
this time of year. He followed up his wire by
a 'phone call in which he told me that there
were other wives in Ambala & as times were so
uncertain he thought we ought to stick together
as long as possible. I packed with some
reluctance, and was incited to rebellion by

4.

every other wife in the hotel and a good few others, all of whom said Harry was crazy to demand that I and the baby should go down from the hills to the plains at the hottest time of the year.

However I packed & down we went, I and the baby and two dogs, and arrived at Ambala at 2.30 a.m. the next morning! The heat here is incredible, and it's the dreariest place imaginable. It was once a very big cantonment, but has been falling into disuse because of a steadily diminishing water-supply. It is full of huge, old, deserted bungalows. There is nothing to do, & there are very few people.

The first thing that happened was that the baby got ill. Something wrong with its tummy and fever. Temperature 105°. A doctor who has only been two months in this country, is very young and so lacking in commonsense as to tell me to put the baby under the fan, " because the poor little thing ~~is so~~ is so hot —!" I replied somewhat tartly that it was sweating profusely, and I didn't want to add pneumonia to its other troubles. To-day is the first day that his temperature has been

5.

normal, but its tummy is not right yet.
One odd thing has happened here, I
ran into Eileen Keegan, one of my
bridesmaids, who is now Mrs. Brown, married to
someone in the Air Force. We have managed to
scrape together a mah-johngg four, and I had
a game this morning, as young Tony was so
much better I felt no compunction in leaving him.
My ayah is excellent, thank goodness. The
monsoon is obviously going to break very soon,
then it will be cooler, so Ambala is not quite
so loathsome as I thought at first. We haven't
the slightest idea how long we're likely to be
here or where we shall go from here, so please
write to me (initials M.M. not H.B.) c/o
Lloyds Bank, Rawalpindi, Punjab, as I have
kept my account open there in case I return
there for the cold weather.

28th June.
Baby all right again to-day, thank
goodness! We were worried stiff about him.
Well, that's enough about us and my
grumbles about Ambala. I know how thankful
I should be to be out here.

6.

Congratulations on the new job. It was a magnificent effort on your part to push off to a new place where you thought you would know nobody. I'm so glad you have found friends there. Wasn't it odd, meeting Jackie Beal there?

Mummy tells me she has gone to stay with Auntie May, but I don't know where! It's surely not the old address at Epsom?

Please send this letter on to Mummy when you have finished with it, and I'll ask Mummy to send her letters on to you. That way, there won't be such long gaps between letters, even if some do go astray, and I'm told the mail is most uncertain these days, besides you never know, now there are Italian submarines to cope with as well.

I enclose snaps of self and Beesknees, with our respective children, also one of ayahs and children. We both have Ghurka ayahs. Beesknees' little girl is a year old. Isn't Tony a little bunch of cuddle?

Much love,

Mary.

19, Elgin Rd
Ambala Cantt.
10th July '40.

My dear Mummy,

I told Phyllis to send my letter on to you, so you won't be surprised at the Ambala address. But I wrote to Phyllis from a hotel. We had an amazing piece of luck and met Eileen Keegan who was one of my bridesmaids in Calcutta. She is now Eileen Brown, married to a lad in the Air Force who is stationed here. She asked us to come and P.G. with them, which we did thankfully, it is so much more comfortable in this lovely big bungalow than in our cramped quarters at the hotel!

Little Tony is quite well again. He has a little prickly heat, but it doesn't seem to worry him, he chuckles and gurgles and plays with his fingers and grows so fast one can almost see him getting bigger! I am the one

2.

who is in trouble now, with impetigo (if that's how to spell it!) all over my face. They couldn't bandage it, so they stuck elastoplast over it, and it was difficult to open my mouth enough to eat! The elastoplast was removed to-day, and my face does seem better.

It has been an appalling hot weather, with the rains hanging about and not breaking, just making it sticky. But we have had a storm to-day which has cooled things down, and everyone has perked up amazingly. We shall soon be moving to Aurangebad, which is further south, but will be cooler because the monsoon has broken there. I don't know how long we shall be in Aurangebad, but after that young Tony and I have decided to go to Bangalore. Two or three of the wives here are going there, so I shall have friends to start with, and by all accounts it's the most delightful place, and healthy for children. I can't tell you where

3.

Harry is going, because I don't know, and wouldn't be allowed to say if I did. I doubt if he knows himself.

Will you please write to me c/o Grindlays Ltd, Peshawar, who will forward all letters to our temporary addresses, until eventually I settle down?

15th July

Just been told I am to catch the train to-night to Aurangabad so must dash off and pack. Harry follows by troop-train.

Much love,

Mary.

Telegraphic Address :
"ENESAR"
Aurangabad.

Telephone No........
Aurangabad.

H. E. H. THE NIZAM'S STATE RAILWAY HOTEL,
AURANGABAD — DECCAN,

20ᵗʰ July '40.

going baths (after a year of tin tubs !!, running h&c, pull the plug & simply marvellous !!)

My dear Flip,

We are staying in the most super. modern, luxury hotel you could well imagine – there's a little picture of it on the envelope, and it's beautifully furnished inside. We are now in Hyderabad State. This is a heavenly place, so deliciously cool after the sweltering heat of Ambala — and green, and there are hills all round. This is Harry's last station before he is sent overseas, and we don't know when that will be. In spite of this, wives were not allowed to go (to Aurangabad) – "because there is no accommodation" – meaning they couldn't be bothered to fix it up! I and a lot of other wives – five in all – have decided that since we are not allowed to be with our husbands, we are going to see the famous Ellora caves at Aurangabad — if our husbands happen to be in Aurangabad, that's nothing to do with us !!! Harry doesn't arrive till to-morrow as he has to use the troop train, which we were not allowed on. The journey here was ghastly, it lasted two days, and we had to change twice, waiting for six hours in a fly-infested dirty one-horse station the second change. I got a two berth compartment to myself which was lucky.

Little Tony is flourishing, and my face is, I think, beginning to get better. At any rate it has stopped spreading and doesn't ooze so much. But there is no skin from under my left eye, down the entire left side of my face round my chin and half-way up the right side of my face! My nose and forehead are free of it, thank goodness. It itches like mad, there are many nights when I get no sleep at all. What terrifies me is the thought, that, it may leave scars! The doctor said I must get away to the hills, but this place is just as good from the point of view of coolness.

Telegraphic Address :
  "ENESAR"
  Aurangabad.

Telephone No.........
  Aurangabad.

H. E. H. THE NIZAM'S STATE RAILWAY HOTEL,
AURANGABAD — DECCAN,

3.

22nd July

     After a couple of days in this place, we have discovered there is damn all to do — not even a cinema to go to. Luckily there are four wives (including myself) who play mah-jongg, so that is how we pass the mornings. In the afternoon Harry often has to go back to work while I read or sleep. But when we have read each others' books there will be no more as there is no library! After tea the baby has its bath and 6 o'clock feed, then we go for a walk. Thank goodness the hotel has a wireless. We listen to that a bit and go to bed early.

23rd July

     Discovered a ping-pong table and the Col. & his wife took us to the golf in their car to play golf. We had a grand game – it's ages since I played & I was awful, still it was fun.

Don't worry over gaps between letters – remember that besides the length of time it takes to get some, letters are often held up in Bombay, waiting for a ship, and censorship also causes delay. I am writing regularly, alternatively to you and Mummy, so if there is a gap, it should be followed by a batch of letters.

Keep on writing c/o Lloyds Bank Murree until I eventually settle down when Harry has gone.

Much love to you all.

Your loving sister,

Mary.

1.

Telegraphic Address :
    "ENESAR"
    Aurangabad.

Telephone No.........
    Aurangabad.

H. E. H. THE NIZAM'S STATE RAILWAY HOTEL,

AURANGABAD — DECCAN,

1st September, 1940.

My dear Flip,

   The dread day has come at last and Harry has gone.
I am not likely to hear from him for some time.

   You are probably wondering why this letter is from
the same address, and not Bangalore, well, I couldn't get into
Bangalore after all. They have started some sort of training
school there, and the place is absolutely packed. I have been
trying to get into Poona instead - I thought it would be such
fun to say afterwards "When I was in Poon-ah - !"; but alas,
it is not to be. Poona is also crammed. So here I am, stuck.
It is very dull here, there are normally only twelve Europeans
here, including the missionaries, but there are a few people in
the hotel now. There is an old doctor who lives in the hotel.
He takes me to the swimming pool after tea every day. Sometimes
I play tennis with Mrs. Mitchell, the manager's wife. The
manager and his wife are a young couple and very nice. I go
for walks and write letters and play with the baby. It is very
dull, but the climate here is good, and I suppose I ought to be
thankful merely to be safe, and to have my baby in a safe place,
away from the dreadful bombing we hear about on the wireless.

   They said on the wireless the other night that Eastbourne
had been bombed and there were several casualties, and I can't help
wondering if anyone we know has been hurt. Isn't it wicked, but
at any rate they wasted a lot of money bombing a place like
Eastbourne! For the most part they don't mention the name of
the place bombed, only say "the outskirts of London", or the
"north-east coast", or something equally vague. I often wonder
about Beckenham. There have been no letters from home for so
long.

   By the way, you notice the figure "1" at the top left-
hand corner of the page? I have decided to number my letters so
that you can tell me which numbers you have received. In that
way we can check up on letters going astray, which I am sure must
happen sometimes. Then if I hear from you and Mummy that letter
No. 5, for example, never arrived, though you have had 6 and 7,
I can look up my notes to see if there was anything important in
No.5, and repeat it to you. As I write alternately to you and
Mummy, you will receive the odd numbers, and Mummy the even.
Don't you think this is a good idea?

Young Tony is growing simply enormous, he weighs over 14 lbs. and I have had to buy some material to make him new clothes! I had some warm clothes for him of the correct size for his present age, because I thought we would be in Murree at this time of the year, but of course he needs cool clothing down here.

This is a pretty place, and there is a delightful walk by the river. At one place there is a stone inscription to say that "These Boulevards were constructed by Col. - (indecipherable) in 1875" - ! It must have been a delightful station in its day.

This place is famous for its hand-woven silks, which are very gorgeous but expensive. There is also plenty of machine-made stuff, cheaper, but I like it better. It also has the advantage of being double width. They have it in all colours with gold medallions worked on it, and others with a closer gold pattern on it. The wife of the manager of the local mill has a housecoat made of some red and gold stuff, and it looks incredibly gorgeous; I'm sure it would make a sensation at home, and when we eventually do get home, I'm going to try and bring some with me for you and Mummy - and Angela, if she's old enough then to wear that kind of thing.

The manager of the mill and his wife are a very nice couple. She is Lancashire, with no pretensions about her, but charming. She runs a creche and kindergarten for the mill-workers' babies; I went to see them the other morning. She says it is hopeless trying to get the mothers to be clean and hygienic, her idea is to get at the children, so that they will grow up in the habits of cleanliness and spread hygienic ideas.

How are you getting on at De Havilland's? I am longing to hear from you. I am sending Mummy's coat care of you at De Havilland's, and Mummy's plans seemed vague in her last letter, and I do not know if it is any good to send the coat to the Beckenham address. I am also sending her some cigarettes, as I hear they are terribly expensive at home, and here one can get an Indian cigarette very cheap, and they are extraordinarily good. I never smoke anything else; they were recommended to us by a doctor, as the purest tobacco in India. They taste rather like an American cigarette, so Mummy may not like the flavour of the first few, but I think she will like them once she is used to them. I will pay the duty at this end, of course.

I hope none of the family have experienced any bombing, it must be terrifying, and it is amazing how well everyone seems to be standing up to it.

- 3 -

Telegraphic Address:
"ENESAR"
Aurangabad.

Telephone No.........
Aurangabad.

H. E. H. THE NIZAM'S STATE RAILWAY HOTEL,
AURANGABAD — DECCAN,

Mrs. Harker (the mill-manager's wife) holds a Red Cross meeting every Monday evening to knit and sew, and I am going to join that, so that I can knit operation socks, or whatever else they give me to do, and feel that I'm doing something for the war, though it will hardly be enough to count! But, alas, it is all that I <u>can</u> do here. Mrs. Mitchell goes, and the missionary ladies.

23ʳᵈ Oct.

To my horror discovered this letter, which I thought had been posted ages ago! I am now in Secunderabad, staying with a Col. & Mrs. Wilmer — otherwise Tom & Sally. They came down to Aurangabad on leave & I made great friends with them & they invited me up here for ten days. They adore Tony. Their daughter has just got married, so I have her room. It seems wonderful here after three months in Aurangabad — so many people about! And they've arranged for a party on Saturday & go the club dance!

I shall wear my black chiffon, and feel quite civilized again! I haven't seen a film or been to a hairdresser for six months — imagine that! I am staying here till the end of this month, then I shall go to Bangalore. A friend of mine is staying at the Central Hotel there — a Mrs. Thurling-Blackwell — and the moment they had a room vacant she had the enterprise to book it for me. I was so pleased. So don't forget — from now on I am at "The Central Hotel" Bangalore — that's sufficient address.

Many apologies — you'll get letter 3 before letter 1! Much love

Mary.

2.

Telegraphic Address :
    "ENESAR"
    Aurangabad.

Telephone No.........
    Aurangabad.

H. E. H. THE NIZAM'S STATE RAILWAY HOTEL,

AURANGABAD — DECCAN,

2nd September, 1940.

Darling Mummy,

I've just remembered it's your birthday to-day, and I never wrote you a letter for it! I'M so sorry, my mind was so full of Harry's going, I'm sure you will understand. Late though it will be by the time you get this, I wish you many happy returns, and hope you managed to have a cheerful birthday in spite of air-raids and such drawbacks! I do wonder what you're doing now.

As you will have heard from my letter fo Phyllis, Harry has gone; where, of course, I am not allowed to know. I am staying on here. It is very quiet and dull, but the hotel is extra-ordinarily good, all modern conveniences and beatifully furnished. And the food is good and the climate reasonable all the year round. So I might do worse. Anyway, I can't get in anywhere, hotels all over India are crammed; I tried to get in at Bangalore and Poona, but both places were packed, and in Poona the hotels are putting tents up to accommodate people!

The mails are delayed, it is a month since I have heard from you or Phyllis. We listen to the news on the Hotel wireless every night, and I heard that Eastbourne had been bombed. What a wicked piece of brutality, there's no military objective there! They often say the "outskirts of London" have been bombed, and then I wonder if they mean Beckenham, so I am longing to hear that you are all right.

There isn't much to do here, there are two other wives with whom I play three-handed mah-johngg in the mornings, and an old colonel with whom I go to the swimming-pool after tea, and every Monday evening Mrs. Harker, the wife of the manager of the local mill, has a knitting and sewing bee for the Red Cross. The other people who go are Mrs. Mitchell, the hotel manager's wife (who is very nice and plays tennis with me sometimes), and two missionary ladies. The Harkers, the Mitchells, and the missionaries comprise the local population! But there are
in/ generally people staying/the hotel, and I believe a new drowd is coming down soon. There isn't even a cinema here!

Young Tony is growing simply enormous. I have started weaning him, he now has one bottle a day. He told me in no uncertain terms what he thought about such a form of cheating during the first day or two, but now he is used to it, and seems to like his bottle. He has "Ostermilk."

2.

I do wish there was something to write to you about, but there really isn't, there are no shops and no cinema, no dances or cocktail parties. Mah-johngg in the mornings, tennis or swimming in the evening, and early to bed after hearing the news! So forgive me for a dull letter. Even if it is dull, I am so thankful to be safe, and to have Tony safe.

Your coat really truly has been packed, insured, registered and posted! I saw to it myself (not much use leaving things like that to husbands, I find). I have addressed it to Beckenham, so I hope you haven't danced off elsewhere in the mean-time!

With best wishes for your birthday
and lots of love,
Your loving daughter,
May.

Telegraphic Address:
"ENESAR"
Aurangabad.

Telephone No..........
Aurangabad.

H. E. H. THE NIZAM'S STATE RAILWAY HOTEL,
AURANGABAD — DECCAN,

2nd October, 1940.

My dear Flip,

Thanks so much for your letter, I was so thrilled to get one after so long, of course the mails are very irregular. All the same I am worried about not having a letter from Mummy for over two months, though I suppose I would have had a cable from you if anything had happened. But Beckenham must be a most unhealthy spot, as we are always hearing over the wireless that bombs have been dropped on the outskirts of London, and they never say just where. I am most worried, I do hope I shall be haring soon.

What splendid news about the job! My heartiest congrats. You jolly well deserve it too, after having the gumption to give up a safe but poor job to go in search of something better. I am glad to hear you are in such a pleasant place, and what it means to be so near the country I can well imagine. In Beckenham one seemed to spend all one's spare time in trains getting to and from work.

I have a friend called Mrs. Leakey who was here and then went to Poona. She is an awful chatterbox, she'll talk about anything at all, just for the mere sake of talking, and she mentioned to a friend of hers, a Peggy Morton, that the sister of a friend of hers had got a job as a buyer in De Havilland's, or rather was being trained as a buyer, and Peggy Morton said "Absolute nonsense, my brother is in De Havilland's, and I know for a fact they don't have women buyers." Mrs. Leakey insisted that it was as a buyer they were training you, and Peggy Morton then said that if it was true, you must be working under her brother. Mrs. Leakey told me all this, but she never asked Mrs. Morton what her brother's name was, so do find out if your boss has a married sister out here!

I wish to that I could show you young Tony while he is still a baby, but alas, there doesn't seem to be much prospect of that. He is flourishing, I have just finished weaning him, and as you know they usually lose weight when they are being wenned, but he gained more weight that month than he has ever gained before in a single month! He now weighs 16¼ lbs., which is 1¾ lbs. more than double his birth-weight. Double his birth-weight is the normal weight for his age, which is just six months. But talk

about weights may show you how he is flourishing, but gives
you no idea at all of his fascinations. He is the sweetest
baby, everybody remarks how good-looking he is, and he never
cries - a little whimper sometimes when he has wind; otherwise,
literally, never.   He has the most delicious chuckle, will go
to complete strangers quite happily, and has the most
enchanting smile.   If he's lying in his cot awake, he doesn't
cry, he plays with his toes quite happily and coos away to
himself.   I do wish there was a good photographers here to
take a really good studio portrait of him.   I shall try to
get some snaps to send you.

The hotel is empty now, except for Col. Taylor, who is a
permanent fixture! - he is the dear old man who takes me to
the swimming pool and for drives - and Major and Mrs. Booth
with their two daughters, Betty and Judy, who are eighteen and
fifteenrespectively, and have just arrived from home.   What a
station for the poor kids to come to!   I spend the afternoons
teaching them shorthand and typing, which passes the time for
both of us, and is being good for my own shorthand which I was
beginning to forget.   There is also a youngster here for the
week, who has certainly livened things up while he has been
here; on two nights we put the gramophone on and danced in
the lounge; three couples dancing - wild night for Aurangabad!!!

I really think I shall have to move to Bangalore, I hear it
is not so full now as when I first tried to get there, I have
been offered accommodation.   The trouble is I shall have to
wait till I have the money for the fare, because the money
Harry left me for the journey was spent on Buttons, the dog
Harry was so fond of, and after all it died.   You wouldn't
believe how much that dog cost, it had to have a peg of brandy
every day towards the end, injections that cost 3 chips a time,
no end of medicines, and tonga fares taking him to the vet.
every day.   And as if that wasn't enough, the infernal dog
got at Becky just before he got ill, and now she is going to
have pups.   Poor darling little Becky, the pups are going to
be much too large for her, and I shall have to send her to a
vet. in Poona who is a marvellous surgeon I've been told, as I
don't think the vet. here is awfully good.   And God knows what
that will cost.   Honestly, dogs are an awful liability, they
invariably get ill just when you can least afford it, I'd
never keep them myself, because I do like to know where I am
financially, and you wouldn't believe the number of times that
Buttons and Becky have got ill and plunged us deeper into debt

Telegraphic Address :
"ENESAR"
Aurangabad.

Telephone No.........
Aurangabad.

H. E. H. THE NIZAM'S STATE RAILWAY HOTEL,

AURANGABAD — DECCAN,

- 3 -

just when we've been hoping to get out of it.   Of course,
Harry will spend anything on a dog, and he has the infuriating
habit of adopting other people's dogs when they get sent overseas.   We have five at one time in Peshawar, a brindle bull-
terrier and a white bull-terrier among them, and we spent half
the day disentangling dog-fights.   Thank heavens we managed
to get rid of all except our own two.

I have had a letter from Harry at long last, and he is all
right.   Their convoy was bombed, he said, "but their aim
was bad."   He is in the Sudan; a beastly spot, I imagine.   He
has a scheme for bringing Angela out if Mummy would agree, but
unfortunately we cannot afford to keep her entirely, and would
have to ask Mummy for something towards her keep.   She'd miss
a lot of schooling I'm afraid.   Anyway, Mummy must decide that,
I am writing to explain it all to her.

By the way, where should I write to now?   You say in
your letter that Mummy is staying with a succession of aunts.
I sent her coat to the Beckenham address, so if she has left
Beckenham, please tell her to write to the Post Office there
giving them her new address.   It would break my heart if that
belated present went astray!

That's all my news.   Keep on writing to me here;   I doubt
if I'll move before Christmas.

Always your affectionate sister,

Mary

P.S. Can't read the address on your
letter!

The Central Hotel,
Bangalore.

15th Nov. 1940.

My dear Mummy,

It's simply ages since I've heard from you, but the letter I had from Teddy about a week ago, took just on three months to reach me, and I hear from other people that their letters from home sometimes take longer, so I expect yours are still on the sea. I am so anxious to hear that the fur coat arrived safely, and do hope you like it.

I didn't realise letters were going to take as long as that, or I'd have written my Christmas mail before! By the time you get this I expect Christmas will be well over, however, I'll wish you all the best for 1941, and hope it sees the end of this dreadful war.

As you see I am now in Bangalore. Aurangabad was so dull, when Mrs. Thruling Blackwell wrote and told me there was a vacancy here, I jumped at the chance. Now I wish I hadn't. It has rained all the time I have been here - since the beginning of the month - and it is deadly dull. And young Tony has had Bangalore tummy, poor little mite. It is all over now, though, and he is as happy and fat and adorable as ever. There really never was such a good baby. I enclose a snap of him with the ayah, which was taken in Aurangabad just before I left. I wish I could send one with me in it too, because I know you'd like that, but unfortunately they didn't come out well and aren't worth sending. Anyway, this one shows you what a little love Tony is. He is always laughing; he is so adorable, I can't imagine what I did before I had him!! The ayah was furious when she saw this snap, she said it made her look like a Madrassi! She appears quite convinced that she is really lily-white. Actually she is a Ghurka.

Eve Thurling-Blackwell and I are thinking of taking a bungalow in Kunoor, which is on the way to Ootacamund (I haven't the remotest idea how to spell it, it's always known as "Ooty"). Kunoor is not so high as Ooty, and gets much less rain. Sharing a bungalow with a friend would be so much nicer than living in a hotel. Kunoor is only 15 minutes in the car (Eve's car!) from Wellington, where there is a club, with tennis, golf, dancing, etc.

It must seem strange to you to hear me talking about being bored, and such petty things as bridge and dances, when you are being bombed. I worry about you awfully, and do hope

- 2 -

you are not getting an awful lot of it in Beckenham, and yet
I can't help realising that it's just the sort of place where
you would get a lot.   Hope they haven't hit the Avenue yet.
And have you got a shelter?   The dug-out in the garden never
materialised, did it?

    Would you like Angela to come out here, and stay with me
out of all this bombing, which can't be too good for a child
of that age?   Because if so, Harry is willing to give up one
of the Lee Concession passages to her, which he has discovered
he can do, and I enclose his certificate permitting this to be
done.   If, when you have thought it over, you come to the
conclusion you would rather Angela were out here, take this
certificate to the India Office and they will arrange things.
We may have to ask you for a little money to help, but we'll
see first how we get on.   If I'm in a bungalow it will be
all right, if I have to have Angela with me in a hotel, it
will of course be more expensive and then I'll have to ask
you for something, though I'd hate doing it.   Anyway, it
shouldn't be as expensive as school.

    Do you know, Teddy is the only one I've heard from during
the last four months?   I keep telling myself that if anything
had gone wrong I'd have had a cable, all the same, I am longing
to have a letter assuring me that you are all unharmed and well.

    Harry seems to be frightfully busy, he told me in one
letter that he was working sixteen hours a day, however, I
hear from him fairly regularly, though his letters are short
and necessarily uninformative.

    My love to you all, and kisses from Tony.

                    You loving daughter,

                    Mary.

263

"Ascot"
26, Grant Road,
Bangalore.

25th April 1941.

My dear Flip,

It's such a long time since I wrote to you that I
~~feel almost~~ ashamed to write at all!   Please forgive me -
I shan't let such a gap occur again, I promise you.

The chief reason for this gap is, that I rashly
became Hon. Secretary and Treasurer to the War Fund
Association here, a job that meant organising about 30
work-parties and handling R⁵.3,000 a month, buying bandage
cloth, gauze, knitting wool, etc., sending in reports to
the Executive Committee, attending Committee meetings at
which I had to take down the minutes - well, anyway, it
was a pretty full time job, and I handed in my resignation
at the last Committee meeting, because I found I was
getting absolutely no time to deal with my own affairs,
and young Tony was getting to know the ayah better than
me.   Anyway, I'm a free woman again now, and am I glad
of it!   And now I must set to work to deal with arrears
of correspondence and incidentally do some mending!

You have repeatedly ask for Harry's address - here it
is:-
            Capt. H.B.Cuerden, R.I.A.S.C.,
                c/o 104, Supply Personnel Company,
                    Middle East Forces,
                        Sudan.

The last time I heard from him he was busy taking Karen -
with a little assistance, of course!   I don't know what
the leave prospects are.   He should get a month in September.

I was so glad to hear from your last letter that you had
been having quite a gay time.   I wish I could have you out
here.   One feels ashamed of oneself out here when one hears
from home, because the only difference the war seems to make
to us, is the difficulty of getting cosmetics!   That is,
it's the only difference for those who have their husbands
with them.   People beat it up as much as ever, and I have
about one early night a week.   Most of my boy-friends are
instructors at the cadet college here.   They are champing
to get overseas of course.

My chief girl friend here is a girl called Gerry Grant-
Cameron, whose husband is a cadet.   They come from the
Phillipine Islands and are most amusing, because they have
got quite Americanised, and are sometimes quite difficult
to understand.

- 2 -

My chief boy-friend is an awfully nice lad in the
Somersets, who is an instructor. He is a marvellous
athlete, and is teaching me to dive. I had my first
lesson at midnight after a dance! I've always funked
going in headfirst, so I think that was a good time to
start, after I'd had a drink of two to give me Dutch courage.
Anyway, he says I show promise, and will be going off the
top board soon. I once rashly undertook to play tennis
with him, and made a perfect fool of myself, because you
know what my tennis is like, and I discovered afterwards
that he had played for his county. His name is Tony Samuda.
Isn't it a weird name? I call him F.J., because I said his
name sounded Japanese. The "F" stands for "feathery",
because his hair stands up over his ears in feathers, making
him look the most awful cissy - very misleading.

I also have a sugar-daddy - Col. Miller-Hallet, whom I
call Middle-Tickle - not because he does, I assure you! -
who takes me sailing. There is a lake about 7 miles out,
where there is a Yachting Club, and sailing is very popular.
It gets quite rough on this lake, and a sail on a rough day
is one of the most thrilling things I know, with the boat
right over on its side. It's so grand to get out there too,
because Bangalore is beastly hot, Bangalore is supposed to
be an all-the-year-round station with a mild hot weather, so
none of the bungalows have fans, and actually it goes up to
about 100° - it's 96° at the moment - and I personally find
it a lot worse than over 100° with fans. Poor little Tony
has absolutely no colour at all, though he keeps amazingly
well and happy and never cries. He now has six teeth, and
he cut them all without any trouble at all, so there can't
be much need to worry about him, even if he is pale.

As a peace-offering for my neglect I enclose two
enlargements fromsnaps - aren't they good? I expect Mummy
would like to have the one of both of us - but keep them
both if you like, because another snap that turned out very
well, is now being enlarged, and I will send it to Mummy as
soon as it is ready. Tell her that, please. I also send
two photos of Harry and me at the Pindi races, goodness knows
how long ago that was, November before last, I think. I
remember telling Mummy that I was going to send her these
photos, and then I lost them, but they have just turned up
and may interest her. I don't look bad for someone about
five months gone, do I? Incidentally, don't you think
your nephew a very handsome lad? He has the most lovely
slate-blue eyes - just like Angela's. And platinum blond
hair.

The big excitement at the moment is the Amatuar Dramatic
Show which is coming off in June, during Bangalore Fortnight.
They are putting on "The Housemaster", and I am to do the

- 3 -

part of Rosemary, the elder of the two giddy sisters.
We haven't started rehearsing yet; that begins next Tuesday.
Won't it be fun?

There is an enormous camp just outside Bangalore for
Italian prisoners, and Ivor Stewart, whom I met in Aurangabad
has just come here and is helping to look after them.   He
invited me and F.J. and Gerry and her husband out to the
camp yesterday evening for drinks.   We weren't allowed to
go near them, but could see them wandering about behind the
barbed wire.   There are 30,000 of them, all very glad to be
caught apparently.   Several of them have said that they now
get more for breakfast than they got in the Italian Army for
the whole day.

Well, pudden-face, am I forgiven?   I'll be writing to
Mummy just as soon as I have that enlargement to send her.
Love to Angela and Teddy.

Much love,

Mary

British Families 110₁
Bangalore
26ᵗʰ June '41.

My darling Mummy,
    I'm sorry I can't answer your cable, unless I can get one of my visitors or a nurse to send a cable for me! And I am most terribly sorry you have had no letters since November, you must be so worried. Also it is very disappointing as I have not only written to you, but sent several delightful snaps of young Tony crawling and standing. I suppose they have all gone down. I haven't written to Phyllis so often, but I sent her a letter about a month ago, with some enlargements. I _do_ hope they get through all right.
    Since my letter to Phyllis I haven't written, as directly afterwards I was carted off to hospital with kidney trouble; they thought it was stone, but luckily it wasn't; it was very painful anyway. I came out of

2   H...pital

hospital just in time to see one of my dogs develop rabies, and what an awful business it was. My Ghurkha bearer was marvellous, he caught the dog & chained it up and later took it down to the vet. I wouldn't have gone within a hundred yards of it! Then the baby, ayah, bearer and myself all had to have anti-rabic treatment, also three other children in the boarding-house who had played with the dog during the infectious period. It was a really ghastly business, fourteen jabs in the tummy, and while you are having them you mustn't drink alcohol or take exercise. Poor little Tony, luckily they decided that for a baby seven injections would be enough. But after the first day he screamed the moment he saw the doctor. The other dogs also had to go into the vets hospital for observation and anti-rabic treatment. Bechy had just had another litter too. The dog that died was one of her first litter. the new litter look as if they may be good dachshunds, but I don't know what the father was. Anyway they are very sweet.

3.

The next excitement after that was the play. As I told Phyllis in my last letter, I was asked to take the part of Rosemary in "The Housemaster". Rosemary is the eldest sister — in fact, the leading lady! It is a pleasant part, and chiefly consists of wearing a succession of pretty frocks. In the first scene the two elder sisters appear in white trousers & jackets — meant to be mechanics' outfit, but looked very snappy! The Society (Bangalore Amateur Dramatic) paid for those, but the other dresses we had to get ourselves. I had to get two new evening dresses (one had to be backless) and an afternoon dress. Luckily I had a brainwave and went to a shop which has just opened here and suggested that as a new shop they might like to have their names on the programme. Of course they jumped at the idea and I got two lovely evening dresses and a very smart afternoon frock at greatly reduced prices. In return they had on the programme: "Mrs. Cuerden's dresses by Rachelle" — which looked awfully professional! They import American ready-made frocks.

4.

We put the play on for three nights and it was a great success. The proceeds went to the War Fund, of course. The last night was the big night, of course, with the Resident, the General and all the local big-wigs there, and flowers handed up at the end. I got an enormous bunch of roses from an anonymous admirer, a beautiful tomato-red suede handbag from another admirer, and a child's tin trumpet! I knew who that was from! It was from "F.J." (Tony Samuda of the Somersets) who is my best boy-friend here. After the last performance all members of the caste went back to the club for a very hilarious champagne supper. I got into conversation with Anthony Duguid, one of the cadets, who had been scene-shifting, and discovered that Joe Underhill's wife was his cousin! It was amusing at this party to see everybody in stage make-up under ordinary lights. The producer, who is a professional, called up for the war, thinks I am a natural actress, and wants me to go to New York after the war to take part

5

in a play he is going to put on there! I told him I didn't think 26 (and it would be more by then) was a suitable age to start a 'stage' career!

The next morning I woke up feeling perfectly awful, but not unnaturally put it down to hangover. However my temperature kept going up and I felt sick to the whole time, so the next day I was removed to hospital. The doctor was convinced it was malaria, & kept taking blood-tests which of course were negative; I was equally positive it was jaundice and told him so. I'd heard so much about jaundice that I recognised the symptoms; lots of my friends have had it, everyone gets it in Bangalore sooner or later. They kept on giving me quinine which of course was quite useless, so I just poured it into a vase by my bed. The flowers didn't like it much either. Yesterday I was a beautiful daffodil colour and the doctor had to admit it was jaundice. I'd be an ideal person to have at home now, my diet allows me no butter and no eggs!

6.

Young Tony is being looked after by Robert and Margaret Matheson, the Scottish padre and his wife. Margaret is a great friend of mine, young, pretty and great fun. They are a most un-padre-like couple! They brought the young man along to see me yesterday, but he wasn't the least bit interested in his mother — heartless little wretch!

News from Harry is good, & fairly regular. I am hoping to be able to tell you soon that he is getting leave; he is nearly due for it, and said in his last letter that leave prospects were good. Won't that be an excitement!

I am sending this letter to Phyllis to be forwarded, as your address seems a little uncertain now you have left the farm.

My love to Teddy and Angela. I'll be writing to Phyllis.

Always your loving daughter,

Mary.

Poems

This poem is untitled, but is included at Author's request

We know that all things must die,
    So we seek while we may
All that springs under the sky
    That is lovely and gay.
Beauty's our object, our aim,
    To be trapped or cajoled,
Caught, like a wild thing, to tame,
    Just to have and to hold;
Beauty, ephemeral, fleet,
    The desire of each heart,
Caught, and forever kept sweet,
    In the net of our art.

So we must wander away
    On our ceaseless pursuit,
Turning to song as we may
    All the beauty that's mute;
Singing of flower and leaf,
    And the dawn-song of birds;
Wearing a cloak for our grief
    That is woven of words;
Singing to bring others joy
    From our hearts' bitter sense,
Knowing this art's but a toy,
    And our game a pretence.

OBSESSION WITH TIME.

When fears are all forgotten and calmed is every care,
And the spirit of enchantment whose advent is all too rare
    Has bewitched the very air;
I hear the beat of flying feet,
I feel the hours haste swift and fleet,
    Ephemeral are all things sweet.

When all anxieties have been allayed,
And all the sweets of life I see displayed,
    Falls the shade.
For all things sweet and all things gay,
Friendship and love, delight in day,
And joy in work and zest in play,
    All these shall pass away.

When joy has vanished, love has died, delight is dead,
And health and hope and happiness have fled,
    And youth itself seems shed,
Then dread despair weighs on the mind,
The seconds slow and weary wind
    Along their way, unheeding, blind.

Ah, Time, flow on and fill the great abyss
Of years that menace, ages without bliss,
    For even this,
This hopelessness and this dismay,
This weariness of night and day,
That seems to be for aye,
    This too shall pass away.

Fairy dancing

The fairy folk are dancing,
        Are dancing on the green,
In lovely shimmering dresses,
        And wings of silver sheen.

Come, watch their secret revels,
        And see them dance and play
Within th' enchanted circle,
        Beneath the moon's pale ray.

Oh, tiptoe to the yew tree,
        And watch with me to-night,
Until they flee with terror,
        From daybreak's faintest light.

NIGHT DRIVE.

The long sweet day was sweetest at the close.

We both were weary: I half in a doze,

As we drove home, drove slowly through the dark.

No harsh sound broke the stillness to corrode

The silent peace· only the winding road

Was there for company, and ghostly trees,

Lit by the scintillating fireflies.

Ephemeral as happy moments, these,

Or phosphorescence that but gleams and dies,

Yet each as lively as a dancing spark:

Like laughing stars that had come down to play,

And dance for our delight along the way.

This poem is untitled, but is included at Author's request

We are the muddle-makers,
　　We are the spoilers of schemes;
Organisation-breakers,
　　Who don't know what it means!
Our juniors are all fist-shakers
　　For ruined hopes and dreams.

With a vision of panthers and glory,
　　One man shall go forth with a gun;
But if we should hear of the story
　　His leave will be stopped ere begun;
He may call us by epithets gory -
　　But he might have shot two to our one!

Since over breakfast we tarried
　　There's no time for working to-day;
We always refuse to be harried,
　　So take those damned letters away!
(D'you see Captain So-and-so's married?
　　A spell of the Frontier, eh?)

Now tell me, what is all this flurry?
　　A Frontier rising? - oh, stuff!
I've told you that I'm in a hurry -
　　Oh, casualties? - well, that is tough;
But surely there's no need to worry -
　　In Simla we're all safe enough!

This powerful poem about God is untitled and included at the Author's request:

They say that God is good - I know not why;

He gives men life, and makes them wish to die.

Tell me in what His vaunted goodness lies!

Unmoved, He sees the torture in men's eyes.

He made the universe and said 'twas well;

Yet having made this world, what need of hell?

How can we thank Him for the curse of breath?

If death should end all - oh, how welcome Death!

For a good and omnipotent God,

    Your plans have gone sadly astray;

If all-powerful truly you be,

    Then whence holds the devil such sway?

Or if good, then how came to be

    The fears and the sorrows of man?

Does it not make you grieve when you see

    How fails your benevolent plan?

Oh, God, much maligned you must be,

    A strange inconsistency's here;

Perhaps good, or almighty you are;

    You cannot be both, it is clear.

A FEAR IN DOWNLAND.

I lay upon the green turf of the Downs,
Forgetful of the dust and strife of towns,
And all around was sun-drenched, golden, fair.
The drone of insects filled the drowsy air;
The incense of warm grass, the cloudless sky,
The rasping song of grasshoppers nearby,
The heady scent of gorse, its blazing gold,
A dreamy spell around me seemed to fold,
For peace breathed through each sight and scent and sound.

But footsteps told me my retreat was found;
The hazy spell was broken; passing near,
Two voices spoke of war, harsh, grim with fear.
They faded, died; and now my dreams are dead!
Where is the glory that the sun had shed?
The downlands still are fair, but for how long?
Will man destroy their beauty, drown their song?
Oh, Downs, will you be blackened, scarred with shell,
Will your sweet peace become a man-made Hell,
Your eerie mists be yet more eerie still,
Bring choking death to every lung they fill,
And with grim red replace the crystal dew?
Downs! will the fate of Flanders fall on you?
Listen! a silver note - a lark's long trill -
Are thunderous guns and screaming shells to kill
A bird's sweet song? No cause can justify
A war in which all beauty, hope and guiltless youth shall die.

Rain.

When the soft air is pure and washed from stain
We learn the loveliness of gentle rain,
And are as grateful as the thirsting ground,
For rain's persistent fall
And murmurous sound;
Monotonous, yet softly musical.
And as we listen, clearly we recall
Days when a misty grey was over all;
We see wide, silver sheets of water spattered
By the long, slanting lances of the rain,
And bright drops scattered
From sodden boughs that rustle and complain;
And loveliest of all, the drops that cling
To wintry branches, naked, glistening;
As if, in pity for the leafless trees,
They covered these
With buds more delicate than the first green buds
of spring.

This poem is untitled, but is included at Author's request

From brazen skies the sun is beating down,
  Pouring relentless light on houses grey,
On bricks and dust, and miles of sweltering town;
  On airless alleys where pale children play;
And back from pavements the white heat is hurled
Yet somewhere there is beauty in this world;
  Somewhere is coolness, somewhere silver streams,
Dim shadows 'neath the shifting green of trees,
And cool, caressing fingers of the breeze —
  Or are these but the fantasies of dreams?

Could I Despair.

Could I despair,
And tell my heart that you will never love me —
        It cannot be —
That thought would put an end to my distress,
        And happiness
Would steal back gently, like returning spring.
        The sun would bring
Sure comfort; spacious downlands, rain and trees,
        Wild, tossing seas,
Music, and long-loved friends, all these would serve,
        If hope, that nerve,
Would set me free to joy in them again,
        Nor throb with pain.
I might forget, and in spring's gladness share,
        Could I despair.

Joy.

Joy is a wind, exultant, strong,
That sings a wild, elusive song,
And whips to ecstasy of waves
Thoughts that were like calm seas.
Oh, wind, that all too seldom raves,
    Wild wind, blow through this do
Scatter gay fancies here and there,
Like coloured leaves from autumn tree
Throw sparkling laughter in the air
    As if 'twere wind-tossed spra
And die not when your force is spe
But sink to whispers of content.

Flying - Fish.

Black bodies catch the sun,
 Give one white flash,
And dip in the cool blue
 With scarce a splash.

In long, low silent flights
 They ~~turn~~ glide and gleam;
Sombre and songless birds,
 Strange as a dream.

West is the wind, and keen and strong
    And throws the spray on high;
I grip the damp deck-rails and watch
    Green water sliding by.

Green as remembered seas of corn
    That once heaved round my feet,
And broke on that white shore where lay
    The spume of meadow-sweet.

4.4.37.

Fireflies.

The long, sweet day was sweetest at the close.
We both were weary; I half in a doze,
As we drove home, drove slowly through the dark.
No harsh sound broke the stillness to corrode
The silent peace; only the winding road
Was there for company, and ghostly trees,
Lit by the scintillating fireflies.
Ephemeral as happy moments, these,
Or phosphorescence that but gleams and dies;
Yet each as lively as a dancing spark;
Like laughing stars that had come down to play,
And dance for our delight along the way.

Easter Island.

The blue Pacific, island-starred,
   Strange stories could unfold,
But one the waves will ever guard,
   One secret ever hold;
One island stands aloof, alone, in stone.
~~With Grouped with a mystery of stones,~~
    Mysterious Easter Isle;
  Where travellers have paused awhile,
  And marvelled and set sail.
     Oh, years unroll
      Your lengthy scroll,
  That we may read the tale!

  Where now is but a waste of sea
  There once was sun-drenched land;
  The foaming rollers on the strand
  Gathered and thundered ceaselessly.
Beyond was tangled jungle, rank and steaming,
That reached to where, upon a distant hill,
A terraced city lay, deserted, dreaming,
White-walled, deep-shadowed, still.

a poet who had drunk the wine
      of praise.

Dear love, I love this gift you send,
Roses, pale presences that blend
With that dim other presence – you,
That haunts me all the long night
Through.
Oh, vanished hours of our delight!
The roses watch, aloof and white,
And soothe, as might a friendly hand
A pain they seem to understand;
And when my memories banish sleep,
A sympathetic vigil keep.

9.2.38.

The Brain Fever Bird

Brain fever, brain fever, brain fever —
                                    brain fever —
Come, the next note is too high,
Start the scale again and try —
Brain fever, brain fever, brain fever.
    Voice that mocks the lads who died
    Pining for their country side;
    (Voice of mirage, heat and dust —
    (Try again, then, if you must!)
    Voice of sweat and pain —
    (Yet again, bird, yet again.)
Brain fever, brain fever, brain fever!
    Swollen tongue and brain afire —
    Drinking only makes one drier —
        (Higher, higher!)
Brain fever, brain fever, brain fever!

Denial.

My love, you called me cold,
   Your eyes watched mine;
Your brave talk grew less bold;
   I gave no sign –
   Dear love! no sign.

You said that in my veins
   Ran ice, not ~~blood~~;
I know that ice restrains
   Tumultuous flood –
   A dreaded flood.

A gift you asked of me
   Which I denied;
Strange that ~~It seemed~~ & you could not see
   ~~But~~ How my lips lied –
   My heart belied.

Stet ~~But~~ I, who know my heart
   Sent you adrift;
For love's sake let you part
   Without that gift –
   That bitter gift

Europe's March Hare.

In March dat merry Month
De vanderlust ist mein,
In 1935 I went
To vortify de Rhine.

In Ninedein Dirty Sigs I quite
Decided during March
To. have a German Plebiscite
Und to de Ruhr I march.

In 1938 I schoose
De Month of March is right
Fur mein zo wunderbar Anschluss
Und another Plebiscite.

Und in der ~~mont~~ March of '39
I tell the world "I crack yer"
Und zo I take vot is not mein
Und swallow Czecho-Slovakia.

Let Neville vear de Ides of March
He studies not "Mein Kampf"
In 1940 I shall gone
To take away his gumpf.

Bound once more to the flowery earth
Bounds once more to   birth
And homely days of rain
How can I reck of loss or gain

Caught back from that strange
                    timeless space
Where the one reality was your face
Which I now shall see no more —
What wonder, earth, if my heart be
                    sore?

The years broke in on the timeless spell
And rapture died as we said, farewell
Oh, the empty days to fill!
And ~~has~~ then ~~aught the pain to still~~

Take back your gifts, oh rich proud earth
~~Take take~~ friends and fire and frost & mirth

The splendid lion & the dove
Take what you w

Let me leave this dreary ~~laughter~~, let me go
Let me ~~seek~~ the silence — slow

To seek from sun & air & wind
Cleansing {fresh} peace, which I shall find
In all {sweet} cool impersonal things,
The joyous flash of fleeting wings,
The red earth & the scented pine
Whose needles in the sunlight shine
Translucent, brittle as spun glass;
        touch of friendly grass,
Oh, let me wander where I will
By forest path or terraced hill
There shall my restless soul be still
Be still my soul be still.

Let us leave this laughter love and go
~~To~~ Let us seek the silence where the rows are
                        slow